Deep Listening

Deep Listening

A Composer's Sound Practice

Pauline Oliveros

iUniverse, Inc.

New York   Lincoln   Shanghai

Deep Listening
A Composer's Sound Practice

Grateful acknowledgment is made to Andrew Taber for permission to reprint excerpts from *Reflections and Research into the Slow Walk*.

Grateful acknowledgment is made to Mohamed Khaldi for permission to reprint excerpts from *What is Attention*.

Grateful acknowledgment is made to Doug van Nort for permission to reprint excerpts from *Noise to Signal: Deep Listening and the Windowed Line*.

Grateful acknowledgment is made to T. J. Szewczak for permission to reprint excerpts from *Posten Kill*.

Grateful acknowledgment is made to Caterina De Re for permission to reprint excerpts from *Deep Listening Retreat, July 1999 Muerren, Switzerland*.

Grateful acknowledgment is made to Maika Yuri Kusama for permission to reprint excerpts from *Deep Listening Koans and the Wizard of Oz*.

iUniverse books may be ordered through booksellers or by contacting:

iUniverse
2021 Pine Lake Road, Suite 100
Lincoln, NE 68512
www.iuniverse.com
1-800-Authors (1-800-288-4677)

ISBN: 0-595-34365-1

Printed in the United States of America

CONTENTS

ACKNOWLEDGEMENTS

I am indebted to all my students over many years of classes, workshops and retreats for their part in the development of Deep Listening practices. Though I provide the guidelines, the practice is collective and enriched by the experiences shared by each individual.

I am grateful to Ione for her constant companionship and her dream wisdom, to Heloise Gold for inviting me to the Rose Mountain Retreat Center where I established the first Deep Listening Retreat in 1991. She has shared the teaching of the Retreats with me and with Ione since 1991. Heloise provides guidance in the wisdom of the body in her teaching. The result of our coordinated teaching is included in this book. Ione's work can be explored further in *This Is A Dream: A Handbook for Deep Dreamers* and *Listening In Dreams: A Compendium of Sound Dreams, Meditations and Rituals for Deep Dreamers*. Heloise's work with Yang style T'ai Chi is available on her video.

I thank the Pauline Oliveros Foundation for providing the platform for developing Deep Listening. Deep Listening® is a registered service mark of the Pauline Oliveros Foundation.

I thank Catarina De Re, Ramon Sender Barayon and Stuart Dempster for their editing, writing and support.

I thank Nico Bovoso for his cover art.

Pauline Oliveros
August 24, 2003

FOREWORD

It was autumn 1988 when I invited Pauline Oliveros to stop by Seattle on her way to California for a concert. I was telling her about the now infamous cistern 70 miles northwest of Seattle at Fort Worden in Port Townsend, Washington. As an afterthought I organized a recording engineer to document what we, along with Panaiotis who was traveling with Oliveros for the California concert, were to do. When we realized we had a CD, a title was needed. With her typical brilliance, in winter of 1989 Oliveros came up with "Deep Listening"[1] while working on the liner notes. The title was very special because it captured perfectly the two primary references of (1) the huge, underground cistern, and (2) the process by which the music was performed. The title "Deep Listening" succinctly recognizes a type of music making that Oliveros has been practicing for many years. It also marked the founding of Deep Listening Band, but that is a story for another time. Oliveros' timely visit to Seattle seemed to be just the catalyst for her to begin organizing in a more direct way what was to become Deep Listening Retreats and, of course, the various related, shorter workshops.

This *Deep Listening: A Composer's Sound Practice* handbook, for a handbook is indeed what it is, comprises a long overdue culmination, a gathering together, of Oliveros' life work in Deep Listening. It is certainly high time the duality of this practical and scholarly information is, at long last, in one place. The reader can take heart knowing that by the time the "Preface" and "Introduction" have been digested, one will be armed with a basic glossary and clarification of meanings. There is also a specific "Glossary" toward the end that can provide the inevitable necessary quick assistance. One can also expect to be amazed at the well organized, detailed, and (if one will) programmed instruction made available. Experienced Deep Listeners, of whom there are many (several have completed the Three Year Certificate Program), will not be surprised at the information contained herein. Indeed, some have contributed appropriately related pieces in "Appendix" and "Commentaries". What will be a surprise, as they read through this handbook, is how they may only now realize the extent of Oliveros' Deep Listening practice.

Throughout this handbook one will see references to healing, through music, meditation and soundings; as one progresses through the various sections there will be regular references to this. Many of the exercises, practices, and the many little pieces seen throughout, offer a healing component. One of the objectives of Deep Listening practice is to achieve and promote health not only for Deep Listeners but also for those with whom a Deep Listener may come in contact. Throughout the handbook there are suggested exercises and pieces for individuals as well as for groups. The therapeutic component is so strong in this practice that one can make a case for it being the primary purpose of this work. There are audio, dreaming, and movement exercises throughout containing either a direct or an indirect healing message or result. Music at the very least should be a restorative, and there are many cultures throughout the world where this component is understood to be synonymous with music making.

As one reads this handbook it won't be long before it is discovered that humor plays a significant role in Deep Listening. There is considerable research demonstrating that humor is healing and otherwise good for health, and the reader can look forward to encountering humor throughout. There is special listening and sounding that take place from time to time in Deep Listening practice that is humorous. These moments are often unpredictable, but they are invariably welcomed and keep what might be temptations to be extremely serious about the practice from getting out of hand. It is important to keep in mind that humor and seriousness are not mutually exclusive. Humor needs to be kept in bounds, of course, but so should seriousness. Heloise Gold, one of the principle team teachers at the Deep Listening Retreats and noted movement professional, includes T'ai Chi and Yoga practice in her teaching. She is also cited—and deservedly so—as one of the primary humor proponents.

Another principle teacher is Ione, acclaimed poet, therapist, writer, and repository of "dream wisdom" (as Pauline Oliveros puts it). She leads sessions in deep dreaming, with particular attention to sound dreaming or sounds within dreams. Although Oliveros is the recognized leader in the Deep Listening arena, one needs to recognize the astounding contributions of her assisting principle teachers, Heloise Gold and Ione. The three of them form a troika of commitment, direction, guidance, organization, support, and teaching of Deep Listening that is at once active, ageless, beautiful, dreamy, energizing, fearless, funny, healing, meditative, moving, profound, quiet, serious, strong, and timely—timely in the sense of providing tools to cope with the increasingly challenging world that we live in. The practice of Deep Listening provides one with a psychological space where one may repair at anyplace and anytime. This handbook provides direct assistance, whether in the context of classes or on one's own, in releasing the creative energy so sorely needed today.

I am blessed to have known Pauline Oliveros for 50 years—five decades as of this year. We have shared much together, and are quietly celebrating this Sedimental Journey (we are always gathering sediment, it seems). Along the way I have had several occasions to observe her compose, devise, guide, invent, organize, perform, teach, and otherwise bring attention to Deep Listening and Deep Listening methodology and pedagogy. I am grateful to have had these opportunities. *Deep Listening: A Composer's Sound Practice* barely hints at the breadth and scope of the topic. Yes, this book is a document of Oliveros' Sound Practice. But as well it becomes a fine tribute to her skills as a teacher of, guide to, and writer about Deep Listening practice. With this handbook Oliveros has written lovingly about The Work, and Process, that she has shown herself to be so dedicated.

Stuart Dempster
Seattle, 5 January 2005

PREFACE

"The first concern of all music in one way or another is to shatter the indifference of hearing, the callousness of sensibility, to create that moment of solution we call poetry, our rigidity dissolved when we occur reborn—in a sense hearing for the first time."

—Lucia Dlugoszewski[2]

Deep Listening is an evolving practice that comes from my experience as a composer, performer, improviser and audience member. My training in music was generally centered on techniques for how to perform and appreciate music of the past. This type of education is generally true for most music students. Encouragement for composing or improvising and appreciation for new music was almost nonexistent in my earliest musical training. Most students do not realize that they have creative potential to make their own music as well as learning to perform traditional music.

I was always fascinated with listening to my environment. From early childhood I have been a listener. I grew up in a time when there existed a very rich and dense **soundscape**[3] of insects, birds and animals in Houston Texas in the 1930s. This soundscape was filled with chirping, rasping crickets, frogs and melodic mocking birds. Sounds of the natural environment still engage my attention.

Now in the 21st Century, that soundscape is considerably thinned out by asphalt, concrete pavements and building developments. Houston still has cicadas in stereophonic corridors as you walk or drive the streets but the frogs have mostly disappeared, leaving their sonic niches unfilled except for the sounds of combustion engines. A modern technological soundscape has emerged.

In high school I became acquainted with inner listening—an altered state of consciousness full of inner sounds that engaged my attention and eventually made me want to compose. At the age of sixteen I announced that I wanted to be a composer. I was in love with sounds and to be a composer was my passion. Never mind that I did not know how to go about transmitting my inner sounds to outer form, I knew that composing was my path.

My instrumental training included accordion and French horn. On my accordion I performed a diverse repertoire including classical, baroque, popular and ethnic music. I played the horn in bands and orchestras—even in a large dance band!

Composing continued, and at the age of nineteen my attempts were finally successful when I managed to write a piano piece in two parts. Listening and notating were intense and a struggle for me. I became more and more absorbed in composing.

Robert Erickson,[4] my composition mentor, encouraged me to improvise[5] my music. I began to improvise and to record the results if I was stuck in writing a piece. Eventually improvisation became a way to get my ideas flowing.

In 1960, nine years after I had composed my first piece, I won the Pacifica Foundation award for my *Variations for Sextet.*[6] Alfred Frankenstein, the music critic for the San Francisco Chronicle, championed my work and my career as a composer was launched.

Through the sixties I became absorbed in electronic music making. With this medium I began to find the sounds that interested me and were most similar to the sounds in my inner listening. Two of my pieces from this period—*I of IV*[7] and *Bye Bye Butterfly*[8] were released on recordings and have become classics of the period. *Bye Bye Butterfly* was named the best piece of the 1960s by John Rockwell of the New York Times.[9]

Validation by peers and critics and the small cash prize from Pacifica Foundation were encouraging and appreciated by me. I was no longer alone with my passion to compose, and I continued. That is why I feel it so important to educate, nourish and encourage young composers today. I also like to encourage people without musical training to engage in improvisation to experience making their own music.

I began teaching electronic music at the University of California San Diego (UCSD) in 1967. I was one of the few who could teach electronic music—a field still relatively new to curriculum in American educational institutions. I established the electronic music program for graduate study at UCSD.

During my tenure at UCSD I taught *The Nature of Music*[10]—a large course for the general student (a course originally devised by my colleague Wilbur Ogden.[11] This course was hands-on. Every student was expected to compose and improvise, even though most had no musical training. It was our conviction that appreciation would develop through participation in music making.

I composed *Sonic Meditations*[12]—a body of work that could be done by persons without musical training. *Sonic Meditations* are based on patterns of attention. In other words these pieces are ways of listening and responding. *Sonic Meditations* is the basis of **Deep Listening**.

I noticed that many musicians were not listening to what they were performing! There was good hand-eye coordination in reading music, but listening was not necessarily a part of the performance. The musician was of course hearing but listening all over or attention[13] to the space/time continuum (global) was not happening. There was disconnection from the environment that included the audience as the music was played. Observing these phenomena prompted me to investigate human attention processes and strategies.

I began with myself. I started to sing and play long tones, and to listen and observe how these tones affected me mentally and physically. I noticed that I could change my emotional state by concentrating my attention on a tone. I noticed that I could feel my body responding with relaxation or tension. Prolonged practice brought about a heightened state of awareness that gave me a sense of well-being.

In 1967 I wrote an article for Source Magazine: Music of the Avant-garde[14] titled *Some Sound Observations*. The article described the journey of listening to what was happening around me and to memories and ideas that were triggered by this listening.
Soon I was involving my students in exercises designed to bring their attention to listening through observation and sounding. Some of these results may be found in *Software for People*: *Collected Essays 1962-1980.*[15]

> "I sit quietly with my alarm clock, close my eyes and open my ears. At this point the curtain rises and the performance begins. My very surroundings seem to come alive, each sound revealing the personality of its creator. There are several sounds, which become fixed in my ear like some "basso ostinato": the continuous whirrings of factory machinery in the distance and the hollow sound of plopping water in a nearby fountain. This background of sound is interrupted by the piercing motif of a bird. A sudden breath of air sweeps across the deck. The pages of my book respond with quick snapping sounds. The door at the entrance squeaks and moans on the same pitch like an old rocking chair then closes with a thud. I can hear the drapery from an opened window rustling against the coarse plastered walls, while the drawing cord syncopates against the window pane".

While still at UCSD I initiated research at the Project for Music Experiment.[16] Meditation Project[17] met five days a week for nine weeks for four hours a day in the winter of 1972 with twenty participants. We studied mind, body and dream practices from a variety of guests and performed pieces from *Sonic Meditations* daily. This research project seeded Deep Listening practice.

I left UCSD in 1981 and moved to Upstate New York. I was attracted by the rich variety of musical activity in the Hudson Valley and the diversity of traditional meditation practices available. I studied Zen, Tibetan Buddhism, Yoga and Taoist forms from accomplished teachers.[18] These studies deepened my understanding and appreciation for meditation and confirmed my own practice as a composer and improviser.

I led my first Deep Listening Retreat in 1991 at the Rose Mountain Retreat Center[19] in Las Vegas, New Mexico, at the invitation of Andy and Heloise Gold. This retreat took place in a lovely mountain area at eight thousand feet above sea level. The Center is in a relatively unspoiled location with very little technological sound intrusion except for occasional jet airliners. There is no local traffic. The location was inspiring for listening.

I committed myself to ten years of retreats at Rose Mountain and developed the forms of practice that are described in this book. Each Retreat lasts for one week and proposes listening twenty-four hours a day. This includes listening through dreaming as well as waking. A period of silence or non-verbal time is included each day.

Teaching with me at Rose Mountain were Heloise Gold (training creative movement, T'ai Chi,[20] and Chi Kung[21]), and Ione (Listening Through Dreaming[22]).

Deep Listening Retreats were also held for five years in Switzerland,[23] one in Canada[24] and one in Washington State.[25] As the number of participants returning each year increased, I answered a request for an advanced level by creating a Three Year Certificate program[26] in 1995. The first Certificates were awarded to six people[27] in 1998. The certificate qualifies the holder to teach a Deep Listening Workshop.

Deep Listening Workshops are held all over the world. Workshops introduce some of the material of the one week Deep Listening Retreat but are more limited in duration and scope. Workshops can be from one hour to a couple of days. Summer Deep Listening Retreats are scheduled in various locations.

My performances as an improvising composer are especially informed by my Deep Listening practice. I do practice what I preach. When I arrive on stage, I am listening and expanding to the whole of the space/time continuum of perceptible sound. I have no preconceived ideas. What I perceive as the continuum of sound and energy takes my attention and informs what I play. What I play is recognized consciously by me slightly (milliseconds) after I have played any sound.[28] This altered state of consciousness in performance is exhilarating and inspiring. The music comes through as if I have nothing to do with it but allow it to emerge through my instrument and voice. It is even more exciting to practice, whether I am performing or just living out my daily life.

I am pleased to be teaching Deep Listening at Rensselaer Polytechnic Institute[29] in Troy New York at beginning and advanced levels, and also at Mills College[30] in Oakland California via virtual presence on-line with video chat and occasional personal visits.

I am also pleased to include essays and quotes in this book by students concerning their practice of Deep Listening.

Pauline Oliveros
June 25, 2003

INTRODUCTION

Anyone can practice Deep Listening. The form given in this book has evolved from many years of this practice in workshops, retreats and classes.

What is Deep Listening?

This question is answered in the process of practicing listening with the understanding that the complex wave forms continuously transmitted to the auditory cortex from the outside world by the ear require active engagement with attention. Prompted by experience and learning, listening takes place voluntarily. Listening is not the same as hearing and hearing is not the same as listening. The ear is constantly gathering and transmitting information—however attention to the auditory cortex can be tuned out. Very little of the information transmitted to the brain by the sense organs is perceived at a conscious level.[31] Reactions can take place without consciousness.

So what is consciousness?

Consciousness was considered an epiphenomenon by the scientific community and not seriously studied until more recently.[32] Consciousness had no location. Furthermore, evoked potentials in the brain appear up to a half-second[33] before the individual is aware of a stimulus. The brain then remembers the stimulus as happening in the present moment or the immediate instant in one's sense of time. So perception in time is an illusion.

So what is consciousness?

Consciousness is awareness of stimuli and reactions in the moment. Consciousness is acting with awareness, presence and memory. What is learned is retained and retrievable. Information, knowledge of events, feelings and experiences can be brought forward from the past to the present. In this way one has self-recognition.

The ear makes it possible to hear and to listen.

To **hear** physically means that vibrations or waveforms that are within the range of human hearing (in frequency typically 16hz to 20,000hz and amplitude 0.05dB to 130dB) can be transmitted to the auditory cortex by the ear and perceived as sounds. However, the word *hear* has many more dynamics and meanings within a cultural history that is continually changing.

To hear according to the Miriam Webster Dictionary can mean "to listen attentively, or that information has been received especially by ear, or to hear somebody or some thing, or to consider something officially as a judge, commissioner, or member of a jury, or to fully understand something, or to attend Mass or hear confession in a Roman Catholic Church".

Listening has very little definition compared to hearing. Though the two words are often used interchangeably, their meanings are different. To listen according to the Miriam Webster Dictionary means "to give attention to sound or sounds or to perceive with the ear, to hear with thoughtful attention, to consider seriously.

To hear and to listen have a symbiotic relationship with somewhat interchangeable common usage.

I differentiate 'to hear' and 'to listen'. To hear is the physical means that enables perception. To listen is to give attention to what is perceived both acoustically and psychologically.

"Hearing turns a certain range of vibrations into perceptible sounds."[34]

Listening takes place in the auditory cortex[35] and is based on the experience of the waveforms transmitted by the ear to the brain. We learn to associate and categorize sounds such as mama, papa, meow, running water, whistles, pops, clicks and myriads more sounds through experience. Many waveforms after first experience are discarded unnoticed without conscious interpretation. Understanding and interpreting what the ear transmits to the brain is a process developing from instantaneous survival reactions to ideas that drive consciousness. The listening process continues throughout one's lifetime.

Physical descriptions of sound properties and listening do not explicate the phenomenal world of perception that takes place in the auditory cortex. According to Stephen Handel in *Listening: An Introduction to the Perception of Auditory Events,*[36] *"There is no sound pressure variation that will always lead to one and only one perception".* Similarly, there is no perception that always comes from one and only one pressure variation.

Physicists then continue to study the nature of physical descriptions of sound and psychologists the perception of sound. Physicists can measure acoustics and pressure waves. Psychologists must measure the experience of the listeners. Thus neither discipline can solve auditory perception. Sound pressure patterns assist hearing but cultural history and experience influences listening.

So what is Deep Listening?

"Acoustic space is where time and space merge as they are articulated by sound."[37]

Deep has to do with complexity and boundaries, or edges beyond ordinary or habitual understandings—i.e. "the subject is too deep for me" or "she is a deep one". A subject that is "too deep" surpasses one's present understanding or has too many unknown parts to grasp easily. A "deep one" defies stereotypical knowing and may take either a long time, or never to understand or get to know.

Deep coupled with *Listening* or *Deep Listening* for me is learning to expand the perception of sounds to include the whole space/time continuum of sound—encountering the vastness and complexities as much as possible. Simultaneously one ought to be able to target a sound or sequence of sounds as a focus within the space/time continuum and to perceive the detail or trajectory of the sound or sequence of sounds. Such focus should always return to, or be within the whole of the space/time continuum (context).

Such expansion means that one is connected to the whole of the environment and beyond.

What's the difference between Deep Listening and meditation?

Deep Listening is a practice that is intended to heighten and expand consciousness of sound in as many dimensions of awareness and attentional dynamics as humanly possible.

The source for Deep Listening as a practice comes from my background and experience as a composer of concert music, as a performer and improviser.

xxiv • Deep Listening

Deep Listening comes from noticing my listening or listening to my listening and discerning the effects on my bodymind[38] continuum, from listening to others, to art and to life.

Deep Listening is a practice and term that does not come from any religious context, even though religious practitioners sometimes use the words. Thich Nhat Hanh is a Zen Buddhist monk whose usage of the term "deep listening"[39] has a specific context as one of the "Five Mindfulness Trainings" that he proposes. This is a compassion-centered listening to restore communication in order to relieve suffering and bring happiness to all beings. Listening (as a practice in this sense) would be training to respond with calmness and clarity of mind. It is a determination and commitment to reconcile and resolve conflicts.

Meditation in all the meanings of the word is found and defined in diverse religions and spiritual practices. Meditation is used in all its rich variety of meanings to calm the mind and to promote receptivity or concentration.

In religious settings, attention is directed to moral and ethical issues, values, beliefs and tenets of the particular faith and to connection with the divine, or a divine being, or beings.

Whether one is dwelling on something carefully and continually, or engaging in a serious study of a particular topic, planning or considering an action, meditation both religious and secular is attention engaged in particular ways. There is emptying, expansion and contraction of the mind; there is relaxation or "letting go" and focus (attention to a point). Meditation implies discipline and control. There is something to practice!

Deep Listening is a form of meditation. Attention is directed to the interplay of sounds and silences or the sound/silence continuum. Sound is not limited to musical or speaking sounds, but is inclusive of all perceptible vibrations (sonic formations). The relationship of all perceptible sounds is important.

The practice is intended to **expand consciousness** to the whole space/time continuum of sound/silences. Deep Listening is a process that extends the listener to this continuum as well as to focus instantaneously on a single sound (engagement to targeted detail) or sequences of sound/silence.

In order to acquire the discipline and control that meditation develops, relaxation as well as concentration is essential. The practice of Deep Listening is intended to facilitate creativity in art and life through this form of meditation. Creativity means the formation of new patterns, exceeding the limitations and boundaries of old patterns, or using old patterns in new ways.

Animals are Deep Listeners. When you enter an environment where there are birds, insects or animals, they are listening to you completely. You are received. Your presence may be the difference between life and death for the creatures of the environment. Listening is **survival**!

Humans have **ideas**. Ideas drive consciousness forward to new perceptions and perspectives.

Sounds carry **intelligence**. Ideas, feelings and memories are triggered by sounds. If you are too narrow in your awareness of sounds, you are likely to be disconnected from your environment. More often than not, urban living causes narrow focus and disconnection. Too much information is coming into the auditory cortex, or habit has narrowed listening to only what seems of value and concern to the listener. All else is tuned out or discarded as garbage.

Compassion (spiritual development) and **understanding** comes from listening impartially to the whole space/time continuum of sound, not just what one is presently concerned about. In this way, discovery and exploration can take place. New fields of thought can be opened and the individual may be expanded and find opportunity to connect in new ways to communities of interest. Practice enhances openness.

The level of awareness of soundscape brought about by Deep Listening can lead to the possibility of shaping the sound of technology and of urban environments. Deep Listening designers, engineers and city planners could enhance the quality of life as well as sound artists, composers and musicians.

Pauline Oliveros
June 24, 2003

DEEP LISTENING PRACTICE

Deep Listening Practice in class consists of a variety of **training exercises** drawn from diverse sources and pieces especially composed by Pauline Oliveros and other Deep Listening practitioners.

Exercises include **energy[40] work, bodywork, breath exercises, vocalizing, listening** and **dreamwork.**

These exercises are intended to **calm** the mind and bring awareness to the body and its energy circulation, and to promote the appropriate attitude for extending **receptivity** to the entire space/time continuum of sound. This kind of receptivity is essential for creative activity in the arts and can be applicable to any discipline.

The same or similar exercises are repeated in each session or class in order for the student to gain experience and learn the practices that are offered. Deep Listening practice is **process training.**[41] Each exercise is designed to set a listening process in motion. Attention to listening and ways of listening that may be new to the student are seeded and cultivated through repetition, practice and discussion.

Repetition of the exercises provides the opportunity to compare experiences progressively from session to session. These comparisons may help to deepen understanding of the exercise and how it relates to listening and how listening relates to art and life or culture. Repetition brings familiarity, and ease with practice.

Although repetition is emphasized, in practice the same exercise is never the same. Each repetition of an exercise invites the possibility of **new understanding** and the **development** of listening as a desirable practice or tool for living, learning and creative work.

Summary of the Deep Listening Class

First hour
>Gathering into the circle
>Question or commentary around the circle
>Standing for energy building exercises
>Breathing improvisation
>Posture correction

Second hour
>Listening meditation (with theme)
>Journal writing (experience of the meditation)
>Extreme slow walk (with theme)
>Discussion with partner of the walk
>Performance of sound pieces

Half hour break
Third Hour
>Rhythm circle

Last half hour
>Dream Sharing or improvisation

Description of the Deep Listening Practice Sessions (Activities)

Gathering of the class into a **circle** in a space large enough to accommodate the group. The circle can be seated on the floor or in chairs. The instructor is also in the circle. A circle formation is preferred as it is an equalizing symbol and may strengthen the understanding that learning comes through shared experiences.

As the group settles into a session, there may be a "**go round**" to answer a question or make a comment such as "What sound makes you feel creative"?

Next the group stands with space enough between each individual to do the physical **warm up** consisting of selected energy building exercises. An inner and outer circle might be required according to the size of the space.

When the exercises are complete, a **breathing improvisation** consisting of breath sounds takes place. Variations may include Toning or sounding improvisations.

The circle then either **sits** on the floor with excellent posture or in a chair for a listening period of twenty minutes more or less. The instructor gives the theme for the listening.

When the listening period is concluded, each person writes in their **journal** about the listening experience for ten minutes or more if needed. The journal is private and is a record of progress for each individual. Class members are encouraged to write in the journal of listening experiences outside of the class on a daily basis. The journal material is an excellent resource for essays or articles.

The **extreme slow walk** is next. Variants of the extreme slow walk are done as experience accumulates. The walk is done with and without music selected by the instructor. The instructor gives the theme for the walk. For example, walking in the desert or walking in a forest.

When the slow walk concludes, **discussion** takes place between partners about the experience of the exercise for about ten minutes before a return to the circle. Highlights are shared with the whole circle as each partner briefly tells something interesting that their partner shared with them. Group discussion of emerging patterns and themes is encouraged.

A Deep Listening **piece is performed**. This may be an improvisation with sounds or a guided improvisation from *Sonic Meditations, Deep Listening Pieces* or *Deep Listening at Mills*. Pieces composed by former and present class members are performed as well.

Rhythm circle with hand clapping, finger snapping and foot tapping. The group progresses from sensing heartbeat and studying reaction time, to clapping or walking a group tempo, to learning complex polyrhythmic patterns and composing for the circle. Composition of rhythm exercises or pieces is encouraged and facilitated by learning and using forms of notation. Notations can be conventional or invented.

Dream sharing. Dreams are understood as a creative resource. Dreams are shared with a partner, and then highlights of dreaming are shared or performed in the group. Class members are encouraged to listen for sounds in their dreams. Dream partners are assigned as support for dreaming.

Discussion and **processing of experiences** is interspersed throughout the class session.

June 24, 2003

Bodywork

Exercise Preparation

Natural Stance

Stand with feet about a shoulder width apart. Shoulders relaxed, soles of the feet connected to the earth, knees a little soft, palms at the sides. Eyes are in soft focus, seeing everything.

Posture

Adopt natural stance. Bring your attention to the soles of the feet. Imagine that you are growing roots down into the earth. Let the roots be your anchoring to the earth. Sense the soles of the feet and let the energy of the body sink into the soles and roots.
Knees are a little soft to promote circulation.
Shoulders are relaxed. Palms of the hands relaxed.
Visit your heart and allow a very pleasant memory to emerge.
Visualize and light up your spine traveling from the tip of the tailbone, vertebra by vertebra up into the scull.
Imagine a golden thread shooting out of the crown of your head to a distant star.
Imagine that the upper part of your body is floating suspended from a star.
Try to balance the feeling of the lower body rooted to the earth and the relaxed floating sensation of the upper body.
Chin is tucked under a bit to help align the spine.
Try to bring your body into this alignment at different times of the day whether you are sitting, standing or walking.

The Exercises

Arm Swinging

Swing the arms forward and back bend at the knees to gain momentum.
This exercise stimulates circulation of lymph and blood especially under the armpits where tension often accumulates and stops energy flow.

Wrap and Slap

Stand with the feet wider than shoulder width apart. Swing gently the hips from side to side to their comfortable maximum stretch, and let the arms follow with the palms slapping the kidney area and side, alternating sides.
Gradually allow the arms to rise until the palm slaps the lung point just beneath the collarbone in front and the adrenal gland to the back above the kidney.

Eyes are in soft focus seeing everything as the head turns to follow the waist and hips turning.
This exercise promotes toning of the kidneys and lungs as well as a kind of massage of the internal organs as the waist turns. The shifting weight of the body also sends a massage to the soles of the feet stimulating the kidney point[42] that is situated between the large toe, ball of the foot and the edge of the foot. This point is called "The Bubbling Brook."

Taoist Face Wash

Warm up the palms of the hands by rubbing them together. Place the palms of the hands over the face and rub vigorously up and down. Each variation is done 9 or 36[43] times each.
Rub the sides of the nose with the index fingers 36 times.
Rub the brow with the thumbs alternating 36 times.
Rest the thumb knuckles on the cheekbones and rub around the eye sockets with the knuckles of the index fingers 9 times.
This exercise stimulates the sinuses and the acupuncture points associated with the liver.
Mouth wipes: Palms of the hands alternately brush the lips 36 times.
Throat pulls: Pull the throat alternately with each hand 36 times.
This exercise stimulates the lymph glands.
Ear area: Using the index fingers flick them so that the cerebellum receives 9 thumps.
Make a V between the index and third fingers and rub the ears 36 times.
Cup the hands over the ears and thump 9 times.
Stick the index fingers in the ears and do a corkscrew motion then flick the fingers outward three times.
Click the teeth together 18 times.
Massage the gums with the tongue.
Swallow saliva down to the dan t'ien or energy center below the navel.

Shoulder and Body Slap with Hanging Out

Place the right palm on the left shoulder and begin vigorous slapping.
Slap from the shoulder out to the palm of the extended arm and return to the shoulder. Alternate to the other shoulder with left palm and right shoulder.
Continue slapping across the chest and down then to the buttocks, down the legs to the ankles and then return on the inside up to the belly and around to the buttocks again, then back to the chest, back of the neck and top of the head. Then brush the energy down the front of the body.
Let the body follow gravity and bend over into a hang out.
Let everything hang out giving the spine a good stretch.
Sense the pull of gravity on the lips and tongue as well as the rest of the upper body.
Make space between each vertebra.
Place the palms of your hands on the back wherever you need the support.
To come back up, uncurl the spine, with the head the last to come up again.

Abbreviated Yoga Sun Salute

Make a triangle with the big toes together and the heels apart—a triangle of support. Hands in prayer position.
This position closes the circuit between many important nerve endings.
Try to sense the feeling.
Extend the palms out with interlocking thumbs, breathe in then bring the arms up overhead and bend back. Then bring the arms up and over into a front bend. Bring the palms of the hands back together and come back up to the starting prayer position with the palms in front of the heart.
Repeat three times.
This exercise gives the spine a gentle stretch and also the internal organs.

Swimming Dolphin (Chi Kung)

Stand with the feet wider than the shoulders. Extend the arms with the palms out and slightly back.
Breathe. Gather energy as you bend the knees and bring the palms forward and open the first charka, continue the motion of opening out to extend the arms again. Have the feeling of opening front and back each time.
Repeat the same motion opening the next chakra, then the third chakra, then the heart, the throat, the eyes the third eye and then extend the arms upward with palms open gathering energy from the universe.

Bring the energy down to the crown chakra then guide the energy down the center of the body and store the energy in the dan t'ien (located below the navel) with the palms. Repeat the whole exercise three times.

Dragon Tail (Chi Kung)

Stand with feet a bit wider that shoulders. Rest the palms of the hands on the dan t'ien. Allow the right hand to rise up to the right, turn the palm up and float it across the upper dan t'ien (forehead), turn the palm over and float the palm past the middle dan t'ien (heart), turn the palm down and float it back to rest on the lower dan t'ien as the left hand rises up and traces the mirror image of the path traced by the right hand. The floating palm is sensing and gathering energy as it passes each energy center.

Good in Bad out (Chi Kung)

Stand with feet about a shoulder-width apart. Bring the palms of the hands forward with the backs of the hand facing each other.
Gather energy as you bring the palms back to the kidneys rising on the toes. Store the good energy in the kidneys; make fists as you gather bad energy from the liver and spleen.
Then shoot the bad energy out with a sound ("*shoo*") toward the floor as your heels return with a thud to the ground.

Flower Breathing (Chi Kung)

Bring the palms of the hands up through center with the backs of the palms facing each other.
Let the fingers form your favorite flower.
Can you imagine that you smell the fragrance of the flower?
Bring the palms down the sides to the kidneys and around to repeat the exercise three times.

The Energy of Rising/Falling (T'ai Chi)

Gather in a full circle with the whole class facing each other. Take natural stance, breathe with palms extended and turned downward toward the earth. Bend the knees down and up six times with the palms rising and falling. Be aware of the whole circle as well as your own as palms rise and fall in unison.

Breath Wheel (T'ai Chi)

From the energy of rising and falling turn the palms to face each other in parallel position in front of you and continue breathing, rising and falling together. The palms rise and fall as if floating in a body of water. Do this six times.

Energy Sphere

Keep the palms extended from the Breath Wheel as if you are holding a ball. Sense the energy field between the palms. Possibly you will feel some tingling sensations or magnetic force field. Massage this energy by moving the palms closer or further apart. Then gradually fold the palms over your lower abdomen to store this energy in the dan t'ien.

Commentary

Ways of listening can be discovered by doing these energy (Chi) exercises. These exercises are for building and storing energy in the body. The exercises are drawn from Chi Kung, T'aI Chi, Yoga and kinetic awareness practices and are modified for Deep Listening practice.

Doing these exercises before sitting for listening or for studying or working can be helpful. If one is depleted, the exercises will help to restore energy in the body. Otherwise the exercises are very helpful to calm and balance mental activity.

Breath

The Exercises

Breath Improvisation

Standing in a circle, bring your attention to your breath. With short or longer puffs of air use the sound of breaths to improvise a playful piece interacting with others for three to five minutes. Try not to vocalize the breaths. Notice any differences that you feel after the improvisation. Also reflect on the rhythms, texture and shape of the improvisation as if it were a composition.

Breath Regulation

Inhale through the nose for the count of 6. Hold for the count of 4. Keep the throat relaxed. Exhale through a small aperture of the lips with a sub vocalization of the syllable 'hahhhh' for the count of 8. Relax and wait for the count of 4 and repeat the cycle. Sub vocalization of 'hahhhh' restricts the epiglottis and helps direct energy to the lower abdomen.

Commentary

When do you notice your breath?

Breathing is the bridge between the voluntary and involuntary—the sympathetic[44] nervous system and the parasympathetic[45] nervous system, the conscious and the unconscious, the inner and the outer.

> "A person can survive without the breath for only five to seven minutes before death".[46]

Fortunately we can go about our daily lives without consciously attending to breathing. Unfortunately this unconsciousness sometimes leads to shallow breathing especially if the body is relatively inactive. As breath reacts to danger or stress, then breath can claim our awareness.

We can change our breathing by attending to it. With awareness and practice we can breathe more deeply and this calms our mind and emotions. It is a good exercise to bring voluntary attention to breath during the day with a question like: "How am I breathing now?" or "How do I feel if I change my breathing?"

There are many breathing exercises from diverse traditions[47] that are helpful for different purposes. Such exercises involve counting inhalations, holding and exhalations, alternate nostril breathing, complete breaths and so forth. Our main purpose is bringing attention and awareness to breath and deepening breath. **Breath improvisation** is excellent for this purpose.

Improvisation is performing something without reference to a text or preparation. Breath sounds of all kinds are used as playful sound resources. Short puffs, long wind like sounds and other variations such as whistling may join together to create a piece of about five minutes more or less. The effect can be deeply felt as breathing returns to normal after the improvisation.

Toning is another way to deepen the breath. Toning can be done by giving voice to each breath usually with a vowel sound held out for the duration of each breath. Vowels naturally facilitate breath extension play. It is said because toning has a direct resonance on the body that it has a calming (and therefore healing) effect.

Sounding is another way to deepen breath. Any kind of vocal sound can be used to improvise. Like the breath improvisation short sounds, long sounds and variations with lip and mouth sounds can create an interesting group sound oriented piece that will lengthen and deepen the breath during the improvisation.

Breathing deeply helps **circulation** and **oxygenation** of the brain. Unrelieved stress produces shallow breathing and oxygen deprivation. In a positive light we need to stress ourselves to overcome inertia and generate power for living. However, we also need to manage stress for our well being when limits are exceeded. Returning attention to breathing at stressful moments can be empowering.

Listening

The Exercise

Sit either on the floor or in a chair.
If on the floor, use a cushion to raise the sitz bones.
If sitting in a chair, feet are flat on the floor.
The legs should be crossed either in full lotus position,[48] or tucked in close to the body with the knees relaxed downward to the floor.
Posture is relaxed upper body, chin tucked in slightly, balanced on the 'sitz' bones and knees.
Palms rest on the thighs, or palms folded close to the belly.
Eyes are relaxed with the lids half or fully closed.

At the sound of a bell or gong listen inclusively for the interplay of sounds in the whole space/time continuum. Include the sounds of your own thoughts. Can you imagine that you are the center of the whole?

Use this mantra[49] to aid your listening:
With each breath I return to the whole of the space/time continuum.

If a sound takes your attention to a focus, then follow the sound all the way to the end as you return to the whole of the space/time continuum.

At the sound of the bell prepare to review your experience and describe it in your journal.

Commentary

The sitting position described for the exercise is common to many meditation practices. However the two forms of attention—focal and global—are directed in Deep Listening practice to sound/silence. An objective is to feel the sharp contrast between the two forms of attention—the clear detail of a sound or sequence of sounds using focal attention and the expansion to multiple sources sounding simultaneously in multi-dimensions with global attention.

It is important to review your listening experience and to compare your prior and after feelings, sensations, intuitions and thoughts and write them in your journal. As experiences accumulate in your journal, patterns of listening may become discernable and progress will become apparent.

Ways of Listening

Forms of Attention

Focal attention, like a lens, produces clear detail limited to the object of attention. **Global attention** is diffuse and continually expanding to take in the whole of the space/time continuum of sound. Sensitivity is to the flow of sounds and details are not necessarily clear. For example, the crowd noise at a baseball game changes when the focal crack of a bat against a ball is heard. If there is a home run, then the voices of the crowd unify from a fuzzy global rumble into a loud focused roar.

The practice of Deep Listening encourages the balancing of these two forms of attention so that one can flexibly employ both forms and recognize the difference between these two forms of listening.

There are many ways of listening to be discovered and explored. Listening is used in innumerable ways. Here are some of the ways:

> "Detection, isolation, and interpretation of subtle variations in a sonic environment…listening in search, listening in readiness, and background listening…highly attuned to direction, timbre, and texture… Confessional—configuration of listening and speaking".[50]

> Lou Gottlieb's secret for listening to non-stop rappers: "Just listen to the melody of their talk, not to the content, as you would listen to a babbling brook".[51]

Sending and Receiving

If you are speaking, singing, performing with an instrument or otherwise sounding, then you are sending. Are you receiving what you send and also receiving the whole of the space/time continuum of sound?

Use this mantra:
With each breath I send sound and receive sound.

Sound/Silence

There is no sound without silence before and after. Sound/silence is a symbiotic relationship. Sound and silence are relative to one another. Time relationships may be instantaneous to very long. Listening to sounds means listening to silences, and vice versa.

There is no absolute silence unless there is zero vibration. Silence means that we can hear no sounds. Silence is the space between sounds.

Palms of Hands

Rub the palms of the hands together vigorously to make them very warm and to energize the nerve endings.
Hold the palms a little apart and parallel in front of you and sense the energy field* between them as if you were holding a sphere or ball. Your hands maybe close together or further apart to perceive the effect.
Massage this ball of energy and gradually bring the palms of your hands to a folded position just under your navel. (Men place left hand under right hand, women right hand under left hand).[52]
Receive the warmth from your palms into this lower body center (dan t'ien)[53]
If you don't feel the subtle tingling sensations, your energy may be blocked by stiff shoulders or other tensions elsewhere in the body. Breathe deeply to release the tension and continue to sense the palms of your hands.

Soles of Feet

The soles of the feet are your connection to earth (even through the floor). The sole is sensitive with many nerve endings and connections to the inner organs.[54]
As you stand, allow energy to flow to the soles of the feet.
Soften the knees and grip the earth.
Follow the sensations that return from the soles of the feet throughout the body. As you grip the earth with the soles of your feet, there is a reaction force—a return of energy from the earth. This reaction force can give you a feeling of strength.
By bringing attention to the soles of the feet,[55] energy can be raised in the body. The reaction force of gripping the earth with the feet in natural stance can help to promote circulation in the body.

Whole Body

As you listen, notice the impact and effects of sound throughout the body.
Notice when you feel sound in your body.
If you are in conversation, receive with your whole body what is being said.

Multi-dimensional Listening

Sounds are both temporal and spatial. As we converse with a partner, there is space between us created by the sound of our voices and the proximity of our bodies. The sound of the conversation can radiate out of the intended intimate space and be heard by others not necessarily included in the conversation. The intimate dimension is overlapping with a more public dimension that we may or may not be aware of. We can hear the dimensions of the space consciously and unconsciously. Simultaneously we may be taking in other dimensions—a dog barking outside, other conversations in the same room, passing traffic and so forth. Our global attention is engaging with numerous overlapping dimensions created by sounds. At the same time we may be imagining what to say next. We then feel the dimension of imagination or memory.

We are giving attention to more than one flow of sound, in parallel or simultaneously, as well as discerning the direction and context. For example, attending to a conversation, music and external sounds that are cues for something to happen, like a siren or telephone, without breaking any flow. Readiness to listen is always present while already engaged in listening.

Dimensions of sound/silence are the space created by the sound/silence, the instant of the sound/silence, the duration, the quality, the relationship between the listener and the sound/silence, the volume and location (actual and perceived).

The depth of listening is related to the expansion of consciousness brought about by inclusive listening. Inclusive listening is impartial, open and receiving and employs global attention. Deep Listening has limitless dimensions.

Attention narrows for exclusive listening. Exclusive listening gathers detail and employs focal attention. Focal attention is necessarily limited and specific. The depth of exclusive listening is clarity.

Listening is a spatial/temporal phenomenon.

Sound/silence is continual.

Listening also may have a kind of secrecy about it. One can listen to others without their knowing it. This is true of radio broadcasts or conversations that happen in a public place, or when someone chooses to listen surreptitiously to a private conversation (to overhear).

Listening Journal

The Exercise

After the listening exercise, describe your experience in writing in a notebook that you keep for this purpose. Give your experience a title. Notice your feelings about your experience and record them. Of course, writing can be replaced by another means of recording to suit your needs (e.g. Tape).

How to Use Your Journal

Your journal should be private, like your own room. This journal is a place to write, graph, add collage, or draw whatever you would like to record. There is no need for anyone else to look at your journal unless you decide that you want to share a part of it or all of it. Your journal is your sanctuary for your listening experiences. Through journaling over time, your experiences in relation to one another accumulate meaning.

Experiences come and go. Some experiences stay with us easily and others disappear quickly. Some experiences pop into mind at odd times like dreams or flashes/visions. Keeping a journal with descriptions and reminders of immediate experiences, memories and your imagination of sounds, can be surprising and rewarding. Recording your experiences can help the development of your memory and imagination for sounds (and silences).

Recording Your Inner Experiences: *Remembering and Remembering to Remember.*

Each listening meditation has unique dynamics, feelings, sounds and sensations that can be described and tracked in your journal. Sometimes you notice very subtle and quiet differences in sounds you thought were familiar. The slightest difference may lead you to new creative relationships. Such material recorded each time you do the listening meditation will give you a record of your progress in the expansion of your awareness and give you the eventual basis for an essay or article.

Even though an experience may seem not worth writing down, your perspective may change later, especially in the context of many different experiences recorded through time. Allow your inner critic to relax and be calm while you have the opportunity to record your experiences without censorship. A word, a fragment, or a paragraph can later trigger your memory or your imagination and yield an enormous amount of information. Your journal can be as non-linear or linear as you wish.

One way to treat your experiences is to review them like a journalist. Be descriptive and be aware of feelings aroused by sounds and the relationship of sounds. Remember that linguistic thoughts are sounds if you choose to listen to them that way. Another way is to think of the experience as a dream.

During your waking or sleeping life, bring yourself to attention with the thought—"remembering and remembering to remember". You might find yourself listening backward in time to a sound that you didn't know that you heard!

Recording Observations of the External Soundscape

Much of the time we focus narrowly on our goals and objectives. In this narrow focus we may discard or tune out sounds that are not yielding what we consider to be relevant information.

Why should we be interested in the sound of traffic, or cafeteria noises, or the din of multitudinous conversations, or garbage cans crashing in the street at 2 am, or a pin dropping in a quiet place?

All of the waveforms faithfully transmitted to our auditory cortex by the ear and its mechanisms constitute our immediate soundscape. Though we may not be of it, we are in it. Extending our awareness as far as possible to include any and all sounds places one in the center of the environment, with presence and relationship to all that is going on. The body is continually sensing and recording all of the information that is delivered to the auditory cortex, even though we may not be conscious of this constant activity. This is why the brain/body knows far more than our mind can process immediately.

Inclusive listening then opens us to all possibilities in the space/time continuum. Depending on our perspective or emotional arousal, or commitment to a goal or goals, we can enter the profound interplay of the universe through sounds.

There may be a surprisingly strong relationship between the inner and outer experience of inclusive listening. Recording the flow of sounds through the space/time continuum like a journalist can promote a deeper understanding of your presence and meaning in the environment. There is always information in any sound that you perceive.

What does it Mean to Collect All Sounds?

The ear is a faithful collector of all sounds that can be gathered within its limits of frequency and amplitude. Sounds beyond the limits of the ear may be gathered by other sensory systems of the body.

Extreme Slow Walk

The Exercise

Moving as slowly as possible, step forward with the heel to the ground first, let the weight of the body shift along the outside edge of the foot to the small toe and across to the large toe.
As the weight of the body fully aligns with that foot then begin the transition of shifting to the other foot.
Small steps are recommended as balance may be challenged.
Maintain good posture, with shoulders relaxed and head erect.
Use your breathing.

The challenge for this exercise is that no matter how slow you are walking, you can always go much slower.

Commentary

The purpose of the exercise is to challenge your normal pattern or rhythm of walking so that you can learn to reconnect with very subtle energies in the body as the weight shifts from side to side in an extremely slow walk.
You may discover the point-to-point connections of movement and/or the merging into the experience of flow.

The extreme slow walk may be practiced any time. Variations that are added in class:
Walk with music.
Walk with eyes closed.
Walk singing long tones—one per breath.
Walk backwards.
Walk with the big toe coming down first then over to the small toe. Weight shifts to the heel. Knees are bent as if stalking something.

Four Modes of Thought

The Exercise

As you listen to a partner or to conversation around the circle, notice the mode of thought that is being expressed.

During the sharing of experiences here are four modes of thinking that we can notice in our discussions:

Sensation

Feeling   Thinking

Intuition

Sensation is the result of experiencing something through the senses. We say that we feel the soft texture of fur, or the warmth of a fire, the depth of the green of spring grass. Sensation is associated with presence and takes place in the present.

Intuition is direct knowing. Intuitive messages and understanding come to us as flights of imagination or in dreams. Intuition is associated with the future. We can project ourselves into the future through our intuition.

Feeling comes about as the result of experience. Feelings develop over time, unlike emotions, which are direct results of actions that take place in the moment such as threats to survival. Feelings are associated with the past.

Thinking is a cognitive activity that involves language and analysis. Analysis draws on the past, present and future.

Try checking on how you are thinking as you listen:

Are you aware of direct sensations? Where do you experience sensation as you listen?

Are you engaged in a daydream as you listen? Are your intuitions presenting you with imaginary situations and activities—are your physical abilities enhanced? Can you fly in your dream?

Are you aware of feelings as you listen? Feelings develop over time, related to experiences. Emotion is more immediate, and quickly changes with information about what gave rise to the emotion. Feeling is more stable once it is established.

Can you analyze your experience to gain facts and knowledge? How can you take apart your experience and put it back together again?
Can you do this and still be aware of the other three modes of thought?

As you notice these modes of thinking in your daily life, note what mode is more predominant for you; or notice if there is some kind of balance between modes. Also try to shift from one mode to another in relation to your listening. Can you discern what mode of thinking someone else is using as you listen to conversation?

Commentary

Four modes of thought are borrowed from a model put forth by C. G. Jung in his book *Memories, Dreams and Reflections*.

Discussion

The Exercises

Partner

Choose a partner after the Extreme Slow Walk. Discuss the experience of the exercise together. Try to use whole body listening as you take in what your partner says.

After a ten-minute period of sharing information return to the full circle. Each partner speaks for the other sharing with the group some highlight of what their partner said that was interesting.

Group

Offer your experience of the exercise. Notice how much information comes from what others say, even if it is a little. Your contribution is valuable to the whole group.

Commentary

Discussion of the experiences is an important part of the Deep Listening practice. Listening can be ephemeral and escape us easily. Discussion with a partner or contributing in the circle can be grounding and help to capture some essence of what you experience in the process.

Rhythm Circle

The Exercises

Heartbeat

Each person detects and then expresses their own heartbeat, first by tapping on the body. When everyone is tapping, then switch to hand clapping. Each person keeps their own heartbeat and listens to the composite rhythms of the group.

60 Beats per Minute (bpm)

From the heartbeat, the circle finds 60 bpm to express a common rhythm by clapping and/or walking in place. After clapping in unison for a while the group walks in place at 60 bpm and passes the hand clap around the circle. Each person is responsible for one hand clap. Practice until the circle can do this perfectly. If one person hesitates or misses, then the next person comes in on time to restore the pattern.

Multiples and Divisions of 60bpm

Walk in place at 60 bpm and clap in unison at 120 bpm, try 180 bpm, 240 bpm 30 bpm and 15 bpm. Practice variations by walking at 120 bpm or 30 bpm and hand clapping at different rates. Practice passing the handclap around the circle at 180, 240, 30 and 15 bpm while keeping the beat with alternating feet at 60 or 120 bpm. Walking can be in place or walking around the circle.

Variations

When the circle masters **60 bpm** and **Multiples and divisions**, then have part of the circle do alternately 180 and 240 simultaneously. All kinds of variations may be improvised or composed by the members of the circle once keeping the tempo (bpm) is mastered and all multiples and divisions are mastered.

Hemiola

Practice clapping groups of three and then groups of two. Accent the first beat of the group. Practice clapping two groups of three followed by three groups of two. The bpm is constant. When the hands are clapping three or two, the feet synchronize with the accent or the first beat. So the feet keep time with the accents. So six beats that move at the same rate can be perceived differently with the addition of accents that cause groups.

The shifting accent pattern is called "hemiola" and is found particularly in African music as well as other musics.

Try one group of three, followed by one group of two for a pattern of five. Try one group of two, followed by two groups of three for a pattern of eight. Try one group of three, followed by two groups of two for a pattern of seven.

Shifting Accents Improvisation

Establish a beat with the feet alternating in place. The whole group claps softly. Each individual accents a clap at will for a shifting polyrhythmic improvisation.

Zina's Circle: Fast Reaction Time

Standing in a circle in natural stance, take hands with your partners with the right palm up and the left palm down. The circle should be close enough that shoulders and arms can be relaxed. Take time to sense the energy between the palms of the hands.

Start and energy pulse from the right hand that travels from hand to hand around the circle as fast as possible. The pulse is a gentle squeeze like a small jolt of electricity. Try to react as instantly as possible when you receive the pulse in your left hand and be sending it almost simultaneously in the right hand. Keep the pulse traveling around the circle for a few minutes. Next add a whisper to the pulse—"*ha*"—so that the sound of breath is traveling with the pulse around the circle. Next add a full-voiced "*ha*".

Typically reaction time for an individual is one-tenth of a second so if there are 20 people in the circle, the time for one cycle should be about 2 seconds. Notice the lapses in attention as the pulse speeds up and slows down. Keep trying to speed up your own reaction time in each cycle of the pulse.

Commentary

The purpose of the rhythm circle is to learn to listen and improvise with rhythms. Heartbeat rates related to 60 beats per minute (ratio), and fast-as-possible reaction time is studied. Fast reaction time is essential to survival. It is also important for responding to a variety of situations and particularly music, dancing and sports. Fast reaction time can increase your ability to discern and refine rhythms whatever the discipline.

The individual learns how to be a part of a rhythm cycle and to express complex polyrhythms. The goal is to be able to detect the tiniest shift in rate of any hand-clap or pulse.

As the group becomes familiar with the potential and possibilities of rhythm patterns, many variations can be attempted and the members of the circle can compose pieces for the group.

Field Recording

The art of sound recording has developed for more than a hundred years from Edison cylinders in the 19th century to magnetic tape in the 20th century to the computer in the 21st century.[56] Fortunately it is now possible to take a portable recording device anywhere to record sounds.[57] The following exercises may be done using a lap top computer with a recording editing program.[58] Recording may be done with the internal microphone however best for better quality an external microphone is recommended.

The Exercise

Make a ten-minute recording. Edit the recording down to the best three minutes. Upload the three-minute recording to the class web site. After listening to the other files on the web site from classmates choose one or more of the files to mix together with your own file to make a three-minute piece.

Give your piece a title. Listen to the results in a composition recital in class. After establishing constructive criteria the class members give each composer feedback on their piece.

After three pieces have been heard, it is beneficial to compare three pieces for similarities and differences—then six, nine and twelve. Before the comparison the titles and composers of each piece are restated.

A Study in Mixed Environments

Record your home environment. Give some attention to placing the microphone in a strategic location. For the piece using other files, use mixing techniques only. Files may be faded in and out as desired.

A Study in Pulses

The natural and urban environments are full of pulses and patterns. Try to record the most interesting pulses or patterns that you can find in your daily environment.

Pulses are repeating sounds. They may be extremely rapid to extremely slow. The pulse may be natural, mechanical or electrical.

Using a variety of processing techniques such as mixing, filtering, harmonizing, phase shifting and delay make a three-minute piece using your own and others files.

Commentary

Field recording is a great way to become more sensitive to sounds. Headphones tend to focus attention on sounds that ordinarily are not in your awareness. When you listen to the environment that you want to record, listen both with and without headphones until you feel that you are capturing the sounds as realistically as possible. Try different placements of your microphone as well.

The compositional elements in **A Study in Mixed Environments** include mixing disparate spaces together to create a new kind of space and to juxtapose sounds in unusual ways.

In **A Study in Pulses** there is opportunity to create unusual polyrhythmic textures by combining varieties of pulses and processing them with effects such as filters, reverberation, delays, envelopes and other possibilities.

Deep Listening Pieces

The range of notational practices employed to present my work as a composer includes conventional staff notation, graphic notation, metaphors, prose, oral instruction and recorded media. Sonic Meditations are notated through prose instructions or recipes. The notations for Sonic Meditations were presented in written form only after many trials with oral instructions given to many different people. Even though Sonic Meditations are in print, I often vary or revise the wording I use to transmit the instructions in new situations.

Such instructions are intended to set an attention process in motion within a participant and among the group that can deepen gradually with repeated experience. A definitive performance is not expected as each performance can vary considerably even though the integrity of the guidelines will not be disturbed and the piece will be recognizable each time.

The central concern in all my prose or oral instructions is to provide attention strategies for the participants. Attention strategies are nothing more than ways of listening and responding in consideration of oneself, others and the environment.

—Pauline Oliveros, 2003

The following selection of Deep Listening Pieces is taken from a variety of sources, situations and places.

Sound Cycles (1994)
by Stan Hoffman

Preparation
Each participant chooses a sound to make during the piece. Always use the same sound throughout the piece. Sit in a large circle.

Leader
Stand just inside the circle of participants holding a small gong or hand bell. Begin the piece by striking the gong twice and then walking slowly around the circle. The next two times you pass the point from which you started, strike the gong once. When you arrive at the starting point again, strike the gong three times to end the piece.

Participants
First cycle—Alone: intend to sound separate from any other sound.
Second cycle—Dialog: intend to sound immediately before or after another sound.
Third cycle—Together: intend to sound along with another sound, sustaining your sound for a long time.

Suggestions and Variations
The first cycle works best if there are not too many people attempting to sound alone. If you have a lot of participants you can either have only some sound during the first cycle or perhaps double the number of cycles, assigning different participants to different alone cycles.

The group could agree on some theme or guideline for selecting sounds. When this piece was first done at the Deep Listening retreat in Washington (June 1995), the participants were given written parts which specified a sound (for example: deer, sun, sky, and everyone's favorite fern), how many times to sound during each cycle, and whether to sound alone, in dialog, or together. This is a good way to handle larger numbers of participants. It also increases concentration because you don't know ahead of time what the intentions of the other participants are as to when to sound or with what intention.

Collective Environmental Composition (1975)
by Pauline Oliveros (1975/1996)

Each participant explores an environment to find a listening place with something interesting to hear and listens for a while.

Each participant invites the other participants to hear their found listening place. There may be one or more places with contrasting sounds.

Each participant finds a way to enhance, nullify or otherwise interact with the sound or sounds that the group goes to hear.

Each participant finds a way to connect all the sounds, either literally, metaphorically or graphically.

A performance agreement is negotiated.

Earth: Sensing/Listening/Sounding (1992)
by Pauline Oliveros

Make a circle with a group. Lie on the ground or floor on your back with your head towards the center of the room.

Can you imagine letting go of anything that you don't need?

As you feel the support of the ground or floor underneath, can you imagine sensing the weight of your body as it subtly shifts in response to the pull of gravity?

Can you imagine sensing the subtlest vibrations of the ground or floor that is supporting you?

Can you imagine your body merging with the ground or floor?

Can you imagine listening to all that is sounding as if your body were the whole earth? There might be the sounds of your own thoughts or of your body, natural sounds of birds or animals, voices, sounds of electrical appliances and machines. Some sounds might be very faint, some very intense, some continuous, and some intermittent.

As you are listening globally, can you imagine that you can use any sound that you hear as a cue either to relax your body more deeply or to energize it?

As you sense the results of this exercise, can you imagine including more and more of the whole field of sound in your listening? (Near sounds, far sounds, internal sounds, remembered sounds, imagined sounds.)

As you become more and more able to use any sound, whether faint, ordinary or intense to relax or energize the body, can you imagine becoming increasingly aware of all the sounds possible to hear in any moment?

Can you imagine allowing yourself to express the sound of your breath as you continue your global listening and deeper breathing?

Can you imagine expressing any sound that comes naturally with your voice?

Can you imagine continuing this Sonic Meditation by sensing, listening, breathing and sounding?

Can you imagine that you are sound?

Deep Listening Through The Millennium (1998)
by Pauline Oliveros

The purpose of this synergistic project is to promote and encourage listening in as many countries as possible in unusual ways or any ways that are creative. It is an invitation to contemplate the nature of listening over a three-year time span (1999 to 2001): to listen to change—listen in order to change—listen for change.

Whatever you are doing could be a part of this project if you are listening. Participation could mean sharing your perceptions on this list as we are already doing, or engaging in a project that you could share.

For example, I have begun early with *Ear Piece* last month in Germany. *Ear Piece* consists of thirteen questions, which explore the difference between hearing and listening. An interviewer asks the questions in their native language, recording questions, answers and ambiences. The material is edited and mixed with another recorded ambience to create a radio piece.

Note

Ear Piece was commissioned by Studio Akustische Kunst and produced at WDR in Cologne by Klaus Schoening. I want to do this piece in as many countries as I can in the appropriate language of each country. Maybe I'll have a big mix down in 2001.

Ear Piece (1998)

by Pauline Oliveros (1998)

1) Are you listening now?

2) Are you listening to what you are now hearing?

3) Are you hearing while you listen?

4) Are you listening while you are hearing?

5) Do you remember the last sound you heard before this question?

6) What will you hear in the near future?

7) Can you hear now and also listen to your memory of an old sound?

8) What causes you to listen?

9) Do you hear yourself in your daily life?

10) Do you have healthy ears?

11) If you could hear any sound you want, what would it be?

12) Are you listening to sounds now or just hearing them?

13) What sound is most meaningful to you?

Environmental Dialogue (1996 Revision)
by Pauline Oliveros (1975/1996)

Each person finds a place to be, either near to or distant from the others, either indoors or out-of-doors. The meditation begins by each person observing his or her own breathing. As each person becomes aware of the field of sounds from the environment, each person individually and gradually begins to reinforce the pitch of any one of the sound sources that has attracted their attention. The sound source is reinforced vocally, mentally or with an instrument. If one loses touch with the sound source, then wait quietly for another. Reinforce means to strengthen or to sustain by merging one's own pitch with the sound source. If the pitch of the sound source is out of vocal or instrumental range, then it is to be reinforced mentally.

The result of this meditation will probably produce a resonance of the environment. Some of the sounds will be too short to reinforce. Some will disappear as soon as the reinforcement begins. It is fine to wait and listen.

Note: *When people gather together for an event, it is a wonderful opportunity to create vocal and instrumental sound experiences that can be performed by everyone. In many traditions vocalizing is used to bring about deep breathing, which promotes the flow of oxygen to the brain. Getting oxygen to the brain can be refreshing, releasing and a good preparation for listening. Sonic Meditations by Pauline Oliveros, Smith Publications, is a collection of participatory pieces 1971-1989 intended to provide both trained and untrained musicians with the opportunity to participate together in sound oriented music which can be made simply and spontaneously. Environmental Dialogue is from this collection and is offered here in the Rotunda to help resonate the Capitol here in Sacramento California.*

We Could (1980)
(November 9, 1980)

When a group is together, each person (after a focus is established, or not) finishes a sentence beginning with "WE COULD…" in as many ways as possible. Time could be limited, or open-ended. The sentences could be recorded or not. The group could vote on subsequent action according to the sentences, or just enjoy imagining what they could be doing.

We Are Together Because (1980)
(November 9, 1980)

When a group is together, each person finishes the sentence "WE ARE TOGETHER BECAUSE…" in as many ways as possible. When there is consensus on the essentials of the group, then each person finishes the sentence "WE ARE TOGETHER LIKE…" (using a natural analogy or metaphor).

Any Piece of Music (1980)
(November 9, 1980)

Everyone answers the following questions in as many ways as possible:

1) If you could write any piece of music, what would you write? Assume that no kind of restraint exists, i.e. time, money, existence of resources or technology etc.

2) How would you achieve it?

Deep Listening Meditations—Egypt (1999)
by Pauline Oliveros (March 1999)

> The following meditations were composed especially for the March process journey to Egypt led by Ione with Andrea Goodman, Alessandro Ashanti and Pauline Oliveros. It was intended that there would be one listening meditation given each day. The meditations should be done one at a time.

Imagine a sound that you want to hear. During a designated time, such as a day or night, take note of when and where you hear the sound.

From the field of sound that you are hearing, select a sound. Focus on it and amplify it with your imagination. Continue to hold and amplify the sound, even if the real sound has stopped. When you are done, scan your body/mind and notate your feelings.

Listen to any sound as if it had never been heard before.

Listening—I am sound. (Try listening to the words in different ways).

If you are looking—what are you listening to or for?

Focus on a sound that attracts your attention. Imagine a new or different context or field for that sound.
Listen all day to your own footsteps.

Where does sound come from?

Imagine that your ears have extended range above and below the normal range of 16hz to 20khz. What could you be hearing?

Can you find an unusual melody?

If you are feeling sound, where does it center or circulate in your body—psyche?

Listen for a heart sound. (Affective)

In a group or crowd can you hear with their ears?

What is the longest sound you heard today?

What is the sound of our group—of belonging—of not belonging? How do you listen to the field sound of the group? What does the leader listen for? The group member? How do you tune in or out?

Center through what is sounding.

If you could ride the waves of your favorite sound, where would it take you?

Are sounds going out or coming in?

Imaginary improvisation: You are holding the possibility of making the first sound.

Sounds are coming and going and yet creating a field of sound.

Where have you heard the most sounds? The most variety? The most diverse?

As you listen, the particles of sound (phonons) decide to be heard. Listening affects what is sounding. The relationship is symbiotic.

As you listen, the environment is enlivened. This is the listening effect.

The Heart Chant (2001)
by Pauline Oliveros

Stand together in a circle with feet about shoulder-width apart and knees a little soft.

Warm up your hands by rubbing palms together until you feel the heat.

Place your right hand over your own heart. Place your left hand on the back of your left hand partner (back of the heart).

After a few natural breaths sing/chant/intone "AH" on any pitch that will resonate your heart. Sense the energy of your own heart and that of your partner over the course of several breaths.

Can you imagine that the heart energies are joining together for healing yourself and others?

Can you imagine heart energies traveling out into the universe as a healing for all victims and toward the end of violence?

When *The Heart Chant* ends, gradually release your palms and bring them forward parallel in front of you. Sense the energy between the palms as if there were a sphere or ball that can be moved around. Then bring your palms to your own center, fold them over and store the energy.

A Series of Mini Pieces (1992)
(May 15, 1992, San Diego)

Only the performer knows that she is performing.

Throughout the semester, these pieces are done in connection with meditations. The performances are a series of examples.

All encounters are to be considered as performances. Principles prevail. What are those principles? What are the examples?

1. Always be moving toward a goal. Always be actually doing something. Never be aimless.

2. Always speak your native language (determine what that is).

3. Always observe your state of mind behind what you do or say.

New Sonic Meditation (1977)

Over a specified time have a randomized cue (or cue synched with a slowly recurring bio-rhythm) and meditators respond with sound on cue.

The New Sound Meditation (1989)

Listen

During any one breath

Make a sound

Breathe

Listen outwardly for a sound

Breathe

Make exactly the sound that someone else has made

Breathe

Listen inwardly

Breathe

Make a new sound that no one else has made

Breathe

Continue this cycle until there are no more new sounds.

Old Sound, New Sound, Borrowed Sound Blue, for voices (1994)
by Pauline Oliveros

Old sound—A sound that you remember from a long time ago.
New Sound—A sound that you have never made before.
Borrowed sound—A sound that you borrow from someone else.
Blue sound—A sound that is blue for you.

First listen inwardly to find your sound to be expressed vocally. Voice each kind of sound—old, new, borrowed, blue—from one to three times within a time frame of about five minutes. Pace yourself by listening to every one and everything. Find a time for each of your sounds. Voice your sound just before, just after or together with some other person's sound. The piece is finished when everyone has used all of his or her sounds not more than three times each.

For Kingston Composers concert
September 29, 1994
Basel

Open Field (1980)

When a sight, sound, movement, or place attracts your attention during your daily life, consider that moment an "art experience". Find a way to record an impression of this momentary "art experience" using any appropriate means or media. Share these experiences with each other and make them available to others.

Sonic Tonic (1992)

Several performers develop ways through subjective and objective testing to express what tone or sound, or combination of tones or sounds as well as a color or colors, masks and costumes is most beneficial for a particular person. Beneficial means that which produces a feeling of well-being in a person. The performers demonstrate an inviting process to the audience.

Individual audience members are invited to participate in a way facilitated by the performers, which results in an orchestration of individual portraits enhanced by sound, special lighting, masks and costumes in a gradually changing tableaux.

Rhythms (1996)

What is the meter/tempo of your normal walk?
How often do you blink?
What is the current tempo of your breathing?
What is the current tempo of your heart rate?
What other rhythms do you hear if you listen?
What is your relationship to all of the rhythms that you can perceive at once?

Scanning—Hearing (1995)

A group assembles to scan the soundscape by listening. When someone feels the impulse to know what others are hearing, a signal such as standing up or raising a hand is made. The group members share what they are hearing at that moment.

Sound Fishes (1992)

For an orchestra of any instruments.

Considerations

Listening is the basis of sound fishing.

Listening for what has not yet sounded—like a fisherman waiting for a nibble or a bite.

Pull the sound out of the air like a fisherman catching a fish, sensing its size and energy—when you hear the sound,—play it.

Move to another location if there are no nibbles or bites.

There are sounds in the air like sounds in the water.
When the water is clear you might see the fish.

When the air is clear, you might hear the sounds.

November 1992
Fairbanks, Alaska

Sound Piece (1998)

For Charles Boone and his San Francisco Art Institute Class
by Pauline Oliveros

In this piece, a sound could come from any sort of sound source. The sound could be shorter or longer, softer or louder, simple or complex but not identifiable as a fragment or phrase of music (from a radio or recording, for example). Each sound used should have its own character. Sounds that are difficult to identify might be more interesting. Sounds that come from unusual sources, methods of activation or locations might have more interest. The sound sources might be visually interesting (or not) and could be staged to enliven the performance space in an interesting audio as well as visual and dramatic design. Sounds could be local or distant with stationary or moving sound sources.

Each person prepares a number of sounds to present within a predetermined duration, i.e. 10 minutes or longer. Each person may have as many or few sound sources as they want. Each person devises their own time scheme and staging for their sounds within the given duration. The piece begins with the first sound and ends when the time is up.

Variation

Sounds are activated before, after or exactly with another performer's sound. The duration of the piece may be predetermined or if time is not limited the piece could go on until the energy is spent.

July 13, 1998
Kingston, New York

Teen Age Piece (1980)

Some concealed—Some in Sight

Long sounds	Calls	Hunter's Calls
Rung Sounds or Sung Sounds		Rhymes
Short sounds	Cheers	
Repeated Sounds		Insults

Partners

June 22, 1980
Sheridan Park, Michigan

Urban/Country Meditations (1988)

Urban

Listen to a roadway—eyes closed—distinguish size shape make of car by the sound—also speed and health of engine.

Country

Sit by the trees—what kind of tree makes what kind of sound?

Cross Overs (1996)

Sound a word or a sound.
Listen—surprise.

Sound a word as a sound.
Sound a sound as a word.

Sound a sound until it is a word.
Sound a word until it is a sound.

Sound a sentence of sounds.
Sound a phrase of words.

April 2, 1996
Evanston, Illinois

LISTENING QUESTIONS

"The world of possibilities is sound"

1   What is your earliest memory of sound? How do you feel about it now?

2   When do you notice your breath?

3   What is attention?

4   Can you imagine composing or improvising a piece based on breath rhythms?

5   What sound reminds you of home?

6   Do you listen for sound in your dreams? What do you hear? How does it affect you?

7   The distinguished historian, William H. McNeil, has recently argued in his book *Keeping Together in Time* that "coordinated rhythmical activity is fundamental to life in society."
    Can you imagine tracking a rhythm pattern in your daily life and writing about it?

8   Can you imagine a rhythm pattern for the rhythm circle with your own form of notation?

9   Can you imagine composing or improvising a piece for voices using attention patterns?

10 What is sound?

11 What is listening?

12 What action(s) is usually synchronized with sound?

13 When do you feel sound in your body?

14 What sound fascinates you?

15 What is a soundscape?

16 What are you hearing right now? How is it changing?

17 How many sounds can you hear all at once?

18 How far away can you hear sounds?

19 Are you sure that you are hearing every thing that there is to hear?

20 What more could you hear if you had bigger ears? (or smaller)

21 Can you hear more sounds if you are quiet? How many more?

22 How long can you listen?

23 When are you not listening?

24 Can you not listen when something is sounding?

25 Try not listening to anything. What happens?

26 How can you not listen if your ears never close?

27 What meaning does any sound have for you?

28 What is your favorite sound? How is it made? When can you hear it? Are you hearing it now?

29 What is the soundscape of the space you are now occupying?

30 How is the soundscape shaped? or what makes a soundscape?

31 What is the soundscape of your neighborhood?

32 What is the soundscape of your city?

33 How many different soundscapes can you imagine?

34 What would you like to have in your own soundscape?

35 What would you record to represent your soundscape?

36 What sound makes you speculative?

37 What sound gives you chills?

38 What sound ruffles your scalp?

39 What sound changes your breathing?

40 What sound would you like whispered in your ear?

COMMENTARIES

I

I was asked how I go about designing or instilling creativity in my students. This was my answer:

The important thing for me is facilitating a community of creative interest. Creativity is inborn—a birthright that is often suppressed by social imperatives. I try in my classes to open the gates so that the creative spirit of the students can flourish. I do this through listening and encouraging listening, sharing and discussion. My students listen by doing field recording, then sharing their files to make pieces. The students also keep journals of their listening experiences.

I hope this helps. So it is not about "instilling"—that would not be free. It's not about "designing" creativity—I don't think that energy can be designed. I believe that facilitating a listening, caring and sharing environment is an invitation to creative work.

Pauline Oliveros
March 13, 2003
Brussels

II

My own beginning work in Deep Listening practices has been primarily inner work, and as such is not something that I chose to open up to the whole list about, even such a nice list as this one! My experience is that DL—for me Is a way of working. When I really listen in this way I hear differently, in the sense that merely being open to listening changes how I perceive sounds, which in turn changes how I listen, and so on in an ever expansive fashion. This is where discernment comes into play.

I think that Deep Listening is found in all aspects of creative work, across all genre boundaries and artistic disciplines. Being heard is incredibly empowering, and being heard can be described as simply being listened to, in all the audible and non-audible ways we communicate with one another. This is how I understanding the meaning of "just" listening.

Monique Buzzarté
July 25, 1995

III
I just wanted to share this little tidbit with you: That overtone singing I learned at the Deep Listening workshop has sure come in handy for pacifying our little Aria (now only 11 days old). If she's a little fussy, I just start in and it grabs her attention right away and she quiets and if I go on long enough, she'll drop off to sleep. I did this at the hospital, when she was less than a day old, and it worked like a charm. Did me good too.

I have a <modest> theory: that good, in-tune (just-in-tune) singing during the early years of a child's life, will result in a highly developed pitch sense in the adult stage…:-)

Yours,

Tom Djll

IV
As others have mentioned, encountering the DL concepts helped focus ideas I already had. This may, however, come from DL once removed, since I got some of the more important and relevant parts of my musical education studying under Dan Goode, himself one of Pauline's students beforehand. (One of the real revelations of my college years came from watching him, when he probably thought no one saw him, out of the college cafeteria window. He was standing in a courtyard repeatedly clapping his hands, turning a few degrees, turning, listening, and clapping again; when I tried it myself later, I was amazed at how the sound would change with each turn.

Joe Zitt

APPENDIX

Reflections and Research into the Slow Walk
by Andrew Taber

The prospect of learning a deeper form of meditation in sound is both intriguing and enticing. It is one that brought me to the eventual enrollment in a class, which, I had no preparation for, and no idea what to expect. I had taken courses at various institutions from leadership training camps to martial arts schools which had taught me a little as to the great powers which meditation holds, but nothing that really dealt strictly with the beauty of calm relaxation and the focus of one or two of the senses on the environment for that very purpose. The various practices to accomplish this have so far ranged from centering exercises, breath compositions, and the slow walk, just to name a few. In particular, the slow walk was very interesting to me. I had previous experience with walking in a sort of meditation, but the meditation was meant to help me focus my body and improve coordination, not to relax and help me become better aware of myself.

Upon beginning the exercise I found that taking note of my movements and trying to slow them down with each step, whilst listening on all that was happening around and maintaining my balance caused me to focus very hard on taking everything one step at a time, literally. The mixture of the soothing music with this was an experience the like of which I have seldom had in the past. It is this, which has sparked an interest to further delve into the meditation practice of the slow walk.

> "A slow walk is a form of meditation. Participants are invited to notice their breathing, to place their feet gently on the ground, to move slowly from foot to foot and to appreciate the "beingness" of things along the path."
> (http://www.shalem.org/walk.html)

As instructed, I began the exercise concentrating on my motion. It was the first time I had really done so for the sake of just relaxing. By feeling the motion

59

of my feet as they rolled from heel, to blade, to the balls and toes, I was aware for the very first time of the very structure and nature of my feet. How well designed they are for walking, and how functional. It was such a soothing and deep feeling. Then I began to notice the presence of sound, the creaking wood floor beneath my feet, the shuffle of socks against the lacquer, and the swish of jean fabric against itself. The drone of the room echoing its rhythm into the background and the eventual wave of music that came from the stereo. All of these auditory elements combined to play as a sort of soundtrack to the act of walking, which was transformed into an art.

> "When you practice walking meditation in the morning, your movements will become smooth and your mind will become alert. You will be more aware of what you are doing all day long. In making decisions, you will find that you are more calm and clear, with more insight and compassion. With each peaceful step you take, all beings, near and far, will benefit."
> (Thich Nhat Hanh, *The Long Road Turns To Joy*)

According to the shalom website, "The idea of a slow walk is to do something from which naturally arises healing, wholeness and peace (shalem and shalom)." It is a way to "cultivate one's awareness" of the world around us. A tool that can help us come to greater appreciate all the wonders and gifts of life. This is not to say, however, that one is guaranteed a deep and moving experience. But Sarah Breathnach in her book *Simple Abundance*, warns against such expectations.

> "Sometimes we expect to experience immediate transcendence and are disappointed when it seems as if nothing is happening. Let go of expectations and life will unfold, step-by-step."
> (Sarah Ban Breathnach, *Simple Abundance, A Daybook of Comfort and Joy*)

Since that class I have done my own slow walk on 4 separate occasions as a means to focus or just clear my mind, and have found that with each successive time, I am able to go deeper and deeper into my relaxed state, to the point where I find it increasingly difficult to "wake up" from my meditations, but not uncomfortably so. And as I have researched more about proper technique and furthering my experience, I have found some very useful and powerful insight into my own abilities.

> "Walk as slowly as you can imagine walking. Then slow down even more."
> (Tarthang Tulku, *Kum Nye Relaxation*)

According to "Expanding Paradigms" of Austin, TX, Walking Meditation is a great way for the beginning pupil to get into the art of Meditation. It is probably the easiest to learn initially and to practice. It helps to develop all aspects of health from spiritual to physical and logic or cognitive. When it is used specifically for people with an aversion to static meditation, it can help assist to break through to new heights of awareness. And it is also beneficial in that it is not setting specific (i.e. you can do it just about anywhere with enough calm and privacy to have a successful session).

Some guidelines they give for beginners are as follows. "Walking Meditation should generally be practiced for between 15 minutes to 1 hour. A 20-minute walking meditation can also be used as a break between two 20-minute sitting meditations, allowing 1 hour of meditation without placing undue demands on the practitioner."

In the beginning, it is probably best to become comfortable first with the exercise. You can do this by clearing a room in your house, garage, private back yard, or any other place where you will be alone and relaxed. It is better that you walk without a particular goal or direction, so long as you are safe and have plenty of room to turn, etc. According to Paradigms, it is much better to "wander aimlessly" so that your focus is on the travel instead of the destination.

Fortunately there is no one "correct recipe" for the meditation itself. While some groups like Paradigms recommend to "start out walking a little faster than normal, and gradually slow down to a normal walking speed, and then continue to slow down until you start to feel artificial or off balance", others (with stronger Eastern ties, such as the Tibetan Monks—"The Path of Mindfulness in Everyday Life, H.H. the Dalai Lama) suggest beginning with a much slower act. They tell of starting with your body at a relaxed standstill, and then speeding up "just enough to feel comfortable, physically and psychologically." This difference in styles is very freeing to the individual or group desirous to use this form of meditation. It allows for those that have a preference to still master the art if they so wish. Some guidelines that are universal to both styles are the need for patience and practice. As with any meditation, it only improves with repetition.

Additionally there are a few key things to be mindful of. First is your balance, because it is impossible to have a successful exercise if you are off and nervous of falling, etc. Second is your breathing, which should be natural and relaxed. Diaphragmatic is the best according to Charles MacInerney, a member of the aforementioned Texas group, it will allow for the most "fluid" breathing patterns, which is optimal for concentration.

That brings up the key to a successful meditation, and that is concentration. Concentration is, above all else, the cornerstone to this exercise. It is what allows you to study your body's movements and feelings, focusing your thoughts, and maintain your balance and breathing. It is important to pay attention to the manner of your strides, and the awareness of your environment. There are many more detailed suggestions depending on your goal for the meditation, but these elements ring true for all.

As I have combined what I have learned over the past few weeks, and kept record of it both in this writing and in my journal, I have gained a much greater appreciation for this art. And, it has broadened my appreciation for that which is new to me. However, it has also given me a little bit of a glimpse of just how little I know and how much I have yet to learn with regards to meditation, deep listening, and myself. And if there is a word that sums up the way to attain that knowledge, I cannot think of a better one than "practice."

Bibliography

Charles MacInerney, et al. "Expanding Paradigms," Austin, TX.
Sarah Ban Breathnach, *Simple Abundance, A Daybook of Comfort and Joy.*

Tarthang Tulku, *Kum Nye Relaxation.*
Thich Nhat Hanh Foreword by H.H. the Dalai Lama, *Peace Is Every Step: The Path of Mindfulness in Everyday Life,* Bantam Books.
Thich Nhat Hanh, *The Long Road Turns To Joy.*

Websites only

http://aiki-jutsu.com/Page7Zen.htm

http://www.shalem.org/walk.html

What is Attention?

by Mohamed Khaldi

There are five definitions of attention in the Encarta dictionary. The first is *concentration*: mental focus or serious consideration. The second is *interest*: to notice or take interest in. The third is *appropriate treatment*: care or tending to. The fourth is *affectionate act*: a polite, considerate or affectionate act. Finally, the fifth definition is *military*: a formal standing attitude assumed by members of the armed forces in drill and often when receiving orders, with feet together, eyes forward, and arms at the sides.

Although these definitions seem quite different, truly I think they can all be traced to the same action, which is to correctly use our five senses. In order to see, hear, smell, touch or taste, one must first *concentrate*, the first of the five definitions. Concentration is using the power of the mind to focus on the external environment through one of the senses. So for example, when listening to a record, in order to hear the record I must concentrate. The second thing I must do is *take an interest* in what I am hearing. Without this, I may be receiving the information through my ears but not processing it through the mind. For example, if I am studying and children are playing outside, I might hear them through the ears, but I will not know what they have said because I didn't take an interest, the second definition. Then, once the sound is processed in my mind, it is important to give this sound *appropriate treatment*, the third definition! This is where probably most people fall short, in that they may hear the record or children playing, but don't give it enough care or tending to. This is where an *affectionate act* may come in. Once the mind has cared about the information received it can act on it accordingly, like feeling certain emotions, or making a decision to close the window on the children's voices. The fifth definition, the *military stance of attention*, is much the same, in that it shows the concentration, receiving input, and caring about the superior officer requiring the stance. The accumulation of all these points creates respect, which is what the military is after.

So if "attention" is the act of using our senses, it begins with the ability to concentrate. Next is the ability to process our external environment through our senses by taking an interest. Third is giving care and tending to the information we have received, then fourth is responding to the information by an affectionate act. The summation of these properties creates respect. In our case, it is respect for what our senses have heard, seen tasted, smelled or touched.

Posten Kill

by TJ Szewczak

During the time that I've been involved in the practice of Deep Listening, I have noticed a significant change in not only the way that I've been listening to music and the ambience of the world around me, but also to the way that I have been creating and thinking about music and sound. I feel that now instead of simply listening to sound, I am instead exploring it—feeling around in all of the crevices and peaks that speckle the surface of any sound or soundscape. I found this particularly useful in a recent project of mine, which documented the visual and sonic fingerprint of the Posten Kill, a local river that traverses the land between Graftonville and Troy. I composed the piece to be a sort of moving wallpaper, complimented by the huge variety of sound that the complete river offered. In this paper I will explore using words the sounds that I heard, the emotions that they sparked, and the effort that I took to try and bring them to life for my audience.

I started to film near where I intended the final piece to end, about 2 miles into Troy by the waterfall at the junction of rt. 2 and rt. 66. The first recording space that I found was near the base of the falls in a small pool that collected in the side of what appeared to be a broken down retaining wall. The combined sound of the powerful falls pounding the river just feet from me and the gentle lapping of the created waves against the broken stone gave an amazing bipolar sound field. It almost sounded like a combination of coarse sandpaper being piped through a megaphone over the sound of an almost empty plastic soda bottle being shaken quietly in the background. A few meters behind this scene is a placid pond, dotted with small islands and broken trees breaching out of the water. I sat on a sandy shore far away from the waterfall, as to not catch any of its sound yet, and set the microphone on the ground just at the water's edge. The resulting sound was a windy plain that was only interrupted by short bursts of children laughing in the distance. After a short while, a flock of geese flew overhead, squawking noisily in the right channel of the mic.

Leaving here I drove a short while down rt. 2 until I came to the first bridge over the river. Climbing down the embankment on the left side, I climbed across a few strewn rocks until I was in the stream and underneath the bridge. This resulted in a most chaotic sound, as the water crashing around the rocks and the side of the bridge reverberated over each other again and again until the air was completely saturated with its sound. To try and capture the sound of the river leaving this spot. I positioned myself just under the bridge, with one-half of the mic facing downstream and the other to the river under the bridge. This creates an interesting effect where it almost feels like your head is being torn upstream and downstream as the sound travels out one channel and into the next. Traveling further upstream, I parked at Shyne Av. and recorded simply the ambience of the river passing by. This point is where I believe the river is moving fastest, and the sound of rushing water permeates the air. I climbed down to the river's edge, and placed the microphone directly over the water, but pointed up. This creates a sort of stereo sweep as the river rushes by—a sound that makes even the charging water seem tame! I found myself next on Creek Road, near rt. 2's second crossing. To compose my final soundscape for this area, I mixed recordings of several locations. First I got an up-close recording of water sheeting over a large rock near the edge of the river. This resulted in a loud bubbling and gurgling sound that had a very deep tone combining with the soft treble of a small group of rapids nearby. A few feet prior to this, the water is very gentle and rolls through a large bed with wide flat grassy banks on either side. I sat next to a tree stump with a white rock balanced on it and simply pointed the microphone upstream. This resulted in a soft hiss as the water slid by to the rapids behind me, with the wind caressing the microphone every so often. Rounding out the recordings of this location was a close-up sounding of the water as it passed through the slower portions of the immediate area. This finished the soundscape with gentle undulations as the small waves slapped the river's edges and passed by.

Traveling past the next few recording locations, I stopped at a small creek by Postenkill Airport. After dashing across a small runway, I found myself right at the water's edge in a sparsely wooded area with tall weeds and an abundance of prickers. At this location I chose to not record the water at all, and instead just held the mic at head level and recorded the few birds that were out on this sunny day. I think that this was one of the recordings that I was most pleased with, as the birdcalls came out extremely crisp and the only other sound is the wind lightly buffeting the microphone. I can still almost feel the sun resting on my face and see the birds hopping through the branches when I listened to it. Going back downstream, I stopped at what appeared to be a popular fishing spot where the Posten Kill is joined by another river as it journeys towards the Hudson. Unfortunately this spot was unusually windy, and I was forced to place the mic behind a tree and sort of point it towards the junction of the river. When the sound of the river wasn't completely drowned out by the sound of the wind crashing against the microphone. The resulting soundscape was very relaxed as you could hear the river slowly running by. To try and get a better recording of this area I traveled about a half-mile down this stream to a point where it was guarded by steep banks. In this area I got a most interesting recording (which is also the sample that I used in my pulses/patterns project) as I tried to get an 'up-close' recording of the soundscape. One location I recorded was a small pile of sticks and leaves that were caught up against the side of the river, but remained clumped together with the water flowing over them. The water shifting over this obstacle seemed to enhance the natural sound of the river's ambience and resulted in an extremely crisp sound print of the river. I think that this recording really captured the ambient beauty of the river the way that I wanted to and was a stark contrast to the rapids I was recording a few miles downstream. You can almost hear how clear the water looks during this recording and the slow bubbles and undulations seem to just naturally roll out of the speakers. At this same location I also captured the sound of the water rushing around a tree that was growing out of the river itself. This recording was very similar to the previous one I did, except it loses some of its depth in the recording, and seemed much more thin than the previous ensnarement of sound.

Moving further upstream and out of the flat grasslands where my previous recordings had taken place. I started to push closer to the source of the river and into the mountains. The first soundscape that I chose was a tiny stream that was about 10 feet away from the main tributary of the river. At this point the river was much closer to its source and the river was dotted with boulders of varying size obstructing the water's path. The section that I recorded seemed to be the main river's floodplain, but still had a small amount of water passing through. The resulting small stream cut its way through the small cracks of the remaining boulders and rocks with a very peaceful fingerprint, but quietly in the background you could still catch audio glimpses of the crashing that the still swollen river caused a few feet away. Additionally I went out into the middle of the main stream and placed the mic directly in front of a large boulder that I climbed on top of. I was really surprised by the resulting sound—the water crashed around the boulder very much as I expected, but the it seemed to be coming at the obstruction in waves instead of a steady torrent. I mixed these two recording in and out of each other when I created my final piece and the wave nature of the main stream combined with the sporadic peacefulness of the small tributary made a large and deep soundscape.

The next recording was what I wanted to be the 'climax' of the piece: the cascading waterfalls by the junction of rt. 355 and Blue Factory Road. I really wanted to capture the full body of this soundscape so I tried a novel way of capturing the sound. Hiking down to the main outcropping that actually peeked over the edge of the waterfall, I lowered the over the edge until I used just about all of the cord and the mic was 10 feet below me. The result was exactly what I wanted it to be—a complete saturation of all the audio space with an intense pounding of water. It sounds almost as if you were standing right in the middle of the falls and the water was crashing down on your head, invading all of your space, not even leaving enough room to breathe. To add even more body to this recording I went down to the base of the falls and just picked up the ambience of the water as it poured over the second smaller falls and subsequently rushed down the river. This picked up a lot more of the treble sound that the waterfall was creating, and complimented the rumble of the main falls nicely. When these two sounds were mixed, they were easily the most powerful recording in the documentary, and provided a wonderful culminating point for the piece.

A short while upstream I made my next recording at another river junction. To record this section of river I hopped across the large rocks that were scattered here and there until I was right in the center of the intersection. I wanted to capture the sound of the two rivers combining right where I was and then their eventual resolution into a larger stream, so I slowly panned the mic in a circle starting at one of the tributaries, crossing over the next one, and then pointing down the main river. The result was a natural pan that lets the listener know what is happening in the river, without even having to see it. Satisfied with this, I drove into the center of Grafton and caught the river in a very different setting. At this point the water had dug a large deep bed through a large meadow, slowly working it's way towards the upcoming rapids. To add variety to the soundscape, I only recorded the ambience of this location, which included a small amount of songbirds, the gentle flowing of the stream, and a small amount of wind battering the mic. The low level of sound at this point provided a much-needed break from the intensity of the previous recordings, and added another peaceful point the piece. To lengthen this serenity, I decided to record a small pond about a mile further upstream. The water in this pond was almost completely still, so the only sound that I recorded was the wind and the distant murmur of Canadian Geese as they rested in the middle of the pond.

Following the river further into the mountains I came to the home stretch of recordings. The first was of the river as it cut its way through the thick woods of the mountains. To record this part of the river, I found a small pool that was being filled by water pouring over a small shelf of rocks and then emptying down a second set of rocks as it continued downstream. This recording was another serene example of the river, and showed a great variety of tones and 'notes' that the water created as it tumbles on its way. I mixed this recording with one that I did a few more miles upstream at a very similar point in the river. Because the soundscape for these two points was so analogous, I wanted them to sound as different as possible. So to record this area, I found a hollow log that was peaking out of the river, but was still partially filled on the inside and had a low amount of flow going through it. By sticking the mic into the hollow portion of this log, I created a soundscape that I can only describe as a sunken ship still being harassed by a small current passing through it. I really enjoy the hollowness of this particular recording, and it created an interesting transition into the recording I had made just prior to it. The final recording that I made before I reached the source of the river was another small pond, except that this one had a man-made drainage tube coming out of it, and a small stream that flowed over a portion of gravel coming out of that. To capture this sound, I simply stood at the pond's edge and pointed the mic in the direction of the small stream coming out of it. The recording gives the impression of a vast space that is only slightly affected by the small stream running out of it.

Finally I had come to the source of the river—Dyken Pond. To portray the quiet nature of the pond, I found a small pile of rocks that were sticking out into the pond from the shore. I put the mic as closely as possible to the rocks in order to record the tiny lapping and sloshing that the water created as waves endlessly washed up and over their obstacle. Now that I was satisfied with this recording, I headed back to Troy to get the final soundscape—the river flowing through Troy and out into the Hudson. This was the only soundscape that I tried to capture the sounds of civilization that were all around the river. Instead of recording from the riverbank, I instead stayed on the bridge that went over the river closest to the mouth. Standing there I recorded the sound of people walking and driving by as well as the ambience of the river flowing underneath me. I think that as the last recording for my piece it was very successful because it showed a side of the river that I had neglected up until this point—the effect that man had on it.

After I had recorded all of this I went back and started to piece the audio that I had recorded together with the video that I had shot. Combined, I thought that they created an interesting interwoven signature that wouldn't have been possible if I had simply used the ambient audio that was always present in the shots. By taking a small part of the sound that was being created by the river and combining that with the overall soundscape it was creating, I feel that I was able to give the river much more personality and interest than many people would have originally thought it had. In other words, I had to listen to not only the whole of the river, but also its parts in order to make this piece work—and without the practice of Deep Listening I don't think that would have ever crossed my mind.

Noise to Signal: Deep Listening and the Windowed Line

by Doug van Nort

I am finding it difficult to put into words my experience of Deep Listening—my experience within the class and how my involvement with the practice has shaped my conscious and unconscious world in this past year. To be at once direct and simple, I should first begin by saying that Deep Listening as a phenomenon has profoundly altered my relationship not only to my sound world but also to the world at large. Ok, so I'll begin with a testimony—something that I was maybe avoiding as a writing tactic, but what apparently needs to be sounded here and now. It is interesting (to me at the very least...) how my approach to this paper writing venture is, at it's beginning, permeated by this newfound approach (even as I have yet to elaborate in any great detail about said approach); perhaps this structural analogy, this self-reflexive moment itself is the only way that I CAN begin.

Should I ask for a restart? I think not. To begin with a beginning and to end with an ending is something that I take for granted; my experience with DL has given me cause to question this method in the pragmatic, formalized essay sense. Myself, I now have a greater sense of continuum in regards to consciousness, and so maybe I have begun saying this long ago—it is just now that the reader chooses to listen through this filtered form. This sense of continuum, for me, will always have reference to some mathematical/structural notion. The continuum: the line, the circle, the plane, the sphere. This sense of the non-finite also has reference to nothing, this lack being itself relative to these constructions. To my mind, these relationships are natural; our observations of them only discoveries of a beautifully correct symmetry. The creation of an imagined symmetry, one that exists in harmony with those natural harmonies that are already in existence is something I value. However, our relation to this cosmic symmetry, and by extension to one another, is a non-linear, non-oscillatory and all around non-sensical system. It is a beautiful schizophrenia that is often feared rather than revered as it is forcibly asked to enter into an unnatural alliance with simply constructed harmony. It is noise. My fascination with this (phenomenon?) is long-standing, but my approach to it as well as my reception of it has changed greatly in conjunction with my Deep Listening practice. This is the underlying thread that will be examined—through reflections on sound and society and drawing from my DL journal entries as evidence of a process.

When I first became involved with Deep Listening it was August of 2002. I knew a bit about the practice through friends and personal research, but didn't have a firm grasp on what to expect. At this time I was about to enter my second year of graduate school, and had been reflecting on the previous year's events. During that year I had further developed my personal sonic aesthetic—I had an appreciation of all things considered to be "noise music". In my own music I attempted to be as harsh, fast moving, loud and as broadband as possible. I felt that this sort of style was somehow reflective of our current world condition, and that it was important for the furthering of what I saw as necessary social revolution: it confronted people very directly with a sentiment of disassociation and even deviancy. It was my belief that through a process of accepting this somewhat "unconventional" art, one could gain further acceptance of the society in which they lived. For this reason I still feel that noise—however we may choose to define it—is important as an art form and as a part of my music. What has changed though, is my approach to it in the context of composition as well as performance. I no longer feel that the loudest, most abrasive sound is necessarily the most effective way to create this feeling of disassociation. I don't even think that it is necessarily "noise", but rather it depends on how this sound is situated within the sound field and it's relationship to those elements that are "natural". Deep Listening helped me to come to this realization in that it raised my consciousness of my immediate environmental soundscape. This was a realization that I could take any moment of any day and elevate it to the level of a "musical moment". Through this listening practice, I began to appreciate those elements of my sonic world that I was most accustomed to and that seemed most identifiable. However, those that were striking in the way that they seemed out of place in the context of the resulting sound field were most interesting to me. Always, their existence would cause some disruption or perturbation of some kind within the whole of the sound field. Focusing on these disruptions became a fascination of mine—could I find the line between the disturbance and the pristine environment? Through this practice I came to a conclusion: these disparate elements, these disrupting sources were noise generators regardless of their timbral quality. It was the circumstances of the situation that defined their role. The noise that they were generating was the perturbation of the original field. It was noise in that it was a disruptive force in the communication that was ongoing within the sound field—reconfiguring it around these newly introduced elements. The line that exists between the original communication and the newly disordered one is where my focus is. That is, our relationship to our sound world is a mediated and filtered one, and I choose to window my focus so that this line is in the forefront. Each point on this line is part of a spectrum—a moment in time that is part of the process that is the shift from order to disorder, from nature to noise. In terms of composition, my newfound approach has been to examine this line. The goal is still to facilitate a "noise experience" that is unique in its lack of concise communication, but now the method is to subtly articulate this lack. I believe that this allows the listener to enter into the moment, experiencing something identifiable and therefore being able to appreciate the unidentifiable as it relates to this. This sort of listening demands patience, which I feel is necessary to truly coming away from the experience somehow changed. It took me time and much of this patience, integrated with Deep Listening practice, to have this realization. I now feel that I need to present composed sound works in such a way that begs the listener to engage with them patiently. Once inside the moment, the articulation of the "noise" elements can be played out, and this sense of disassociation that I am after can be internalized.

As I said, this new shift in perspective that I have had is a process that has occurred during my involvement with Deep Listening. During some early listening meditations, I would find myself associating sonic elements with other images or with "music". On 9/6 I had this to say: "…I was inundated with concerns and reflections, which either turned from images to sounds or sounds to images. This focus on language and symbols made me (I believe) perceive more of the ideal than of the real. I thought of concerns for the health of people in my life…this led to an awareness of my inattentiveness to my surroundings and a sound like metal and glass (broken) tumbling down a hill towards me…" A reference to a composed musical experience can be seen on 9/20: "…it began that way for me—sounds of water flowing, but in a constant yet abrupt change of speeds (reminding me of Debussy's *Soiree Dans Grenade*)…". I do not mean to imply that a sound experience should not trigger a past experience. On the contrary, I recall the sonic events of 9/20 as being a beautiful moment of water-like environments and this imagined piece by Debussy (one my favorites…) It seemed, though, in those earlier days that there would always be an image/symbol/sound association. If we look to later journal entries, this is not necessarily the case. On 3/26 for example: "Very quiet and equidynamic today. Made for an interesting field. The siren in the distance—before it got close with it's blaring horn—sounded like voices. The two pitches of the siren sounded like two people responding to one another with drawn out (long) tones. I thought this was amazingly fitting, considering the 'mirror' concept that Pauline introduced today…". Clearly there was reference to a symbol (people's voices), but I differentiate this sort of entry because it was not associated with a mental image. Instead it was the sound quality of a human voice that I thought of, and the experience on this occasion was generated internally. That is, all of the dialogue that this sonic moment created was due to the SOUND ITSELF rather than bringing in some outside point of reference.

It amazes me sometimes when I reflect upon my relationship to my sound world now at this moment in May of 2003. I have somehow kept the same sorts of interests and concerns in terms of art and its social function. However, my approach to it and my reception of it is so vastly different that it cannot help but change the art-making process for the better, thereby improving its ability to weave itself into the larger social fabric in a nondestructive way. Further, I think that while concern for global salvation is important, we first need to be connected as a people on a more immediate level. To be in touch with our neighbor we need to be in touch with ourselves and our surroundings. One key factor is our sonic environment—something that connects us as people. Practices such as Deep Listening facilitate this connection in that it allows for introspection, and also that it brings people closer to the fabric that binds them through a common experience.

THANK YOU Pauline for giving me this opportunity!!!!!!

Deep Listening Retreat

July 1999
Muerren, Switzerland
with:
Pauline Oliveros, composer
Heloise Gold, T'ai Chi and creative movement specialist
and Ione, poet, playwright, dream specialist

by Caterina De Re

What is Deep Listening?

Deep Listening® (DL) is a practice created by Pauline Oliveros to enhance her creative work and to engage with others. This practice evolved out of Oliveros' childhood fascination with sounds, and from her work in composition, improvisation and electro-acoustics. It is her commitment to the community at large that includes ways to unite creative practice and daily life. The whole gamut of sound, and the processing of what one hears, is revealed through exercises that re-connect participants with their innate creative potential and the wider environment in a practical, and natural way. Simply put—sound is energy.

These exercises work both body and mind energies to trip up one's creative processes as well as directing one's attention to the interconnectedness of living systems.

The workshop is aptly referred to as a "retreat". Although not free of tourist traffic, the remoteness of Muerren in the Swiss Alps provided a suitable retreat environment. There was an on—going emphasis on meditation and body-awareness techniques that include Eastern and indigenous sources. Fifty years ago German-born Tibetan Buddhist, Lama Govinda, wrote "Art and meditation are creative states of the human mind". Deep Listening definitely adheres to such openness of the mind's potential and sets the context for applying various meditation and movement methods to creative and everyday life. In accordance with the atmosphere of openness, the process was made available without specific cultural or religious bias.

Besides the expected coterie of musicians, performers and sound artists, this workshop attracted music therapists, organizers, administrators, teachers, office workers etc. Whoever is willing to challenge her/his systems of perception through unlocking creative doorways is most welcome. Age is not a question: these workshops could accommodate teens to grannies (and apparently have).

Ollie what's-his-name?

Perhaps it is just to include a little introduction to Oliveros at this point (even "little" does injustice for her contribution has been significant). But, it seems, like many women composers in this vein, she remains less known than her male colleagues. Fellow composer, Larry Austin, offers his tribute:

> Pauline's work and advanced musical concepts were well known and appreciated in the San Francisco Bay Area in the late 'fifties and increasingly in the 'sixties. Her prose piece/poem "Some Sound Observations" was first published in Source in January 1968. She was then and remains a great influence on my own work. [John] Cage appreciated her importance as well and collaborated with her in many, many projects and performances. She continues to make important contributions to the welfare of the new music and avant garde community of artists and human beings.

Listening beyond the "Om"

Training with Oliveros, Ione and Gold was by the far the most challenging, unpretentious, and applicable workshops I have experienced to date. Essentially: their "special teaching method" is one of kindness and pure love of sound in all its variant forms. One personal yardstick to measure benefit is the humor factor and this workshop was full of so much laughter that it still amazes me—given the fact at least half of our time was spent in silence (from late evening to the following day at lunchtime)!

As my own work is deepening sound art through integration of meditation practice, I found this opportunity to train and perform in such an environment of utmost value. Of particular interest to me is the investigation and practice of Tibetan Buddhist "technologies of consciousness". The endeavor to be mindful of this practice naturally extends to my work as an improvising vocalist and composer (or at least, I attempt integration). During my Master's I ventured more seriously into the computer-based technologies of sound. As Oliveros is the Meisterin of both "technologies", there was ample support and understanding from all trainers to grasp the interdisciplinary paradigms I am evolving, and for me to trust the Deep Listening work process.

When Oliveros speaks of her own experience, she refers to the delightful term—"seed practice". For me this term has an undertone to an aspect of Tibetan Buddhist meditation that focuses. The point all trainers make is never to limit the practice to a tradition—rather, make something one's own and expand it outwards. In her own words at the Retreat, Oliveros explains the essence of her practice:

> My own core practice—seed practice—began about 45 years ago, and probably longer than that but the consciousness of it began about 45 years ago of listening—to everything all the time. Reminding myself when I was not listening, and I keep practicing this all the time. And I keep catching myself and bringing myself to consciousness. Hearing is something that happens to us because we have ears—it is our primary sense organ. Listening is something we develop and cultivate our whole life, and maybe all of our lifetimes. Listening is what creates culture. Listening is very diverse and takes many different forms as cultures take many different forms.

Training: bodywork out—working out the mind

Alarm rings before 6 a.m. Listen. Silence. Coffee fix. Dig that mountain view. Walking meditation up steep slopes. Cows bells ding-dinging. Silence. Breakfast. DL training. Sitting meditation. Voiced meditation. Drawing. Writing. Visualization. Improvisation. The trip to have without leaving the room. Lunch. Talk again! T'ai Chi, Qi Qong, dance, move it. Dinner. DL training. Ione takes us to the never-never.[59] Shut eye. Silence. Listen.

Oliveros' partners-in-training, Ione and Heliose Gold, provided a vital role in imparting the mind-body exercises. Gold has adapted Chinese movement (T'ai Chi and Qi Qong) and her own 25 years of dance experience to focus internal body energies. Gold took us through a gentle and meticulous movement series, and often had us bent over double—in laughter! As the workshop progressed, we became more attuned to sensing the connection between our very bodies, consciousness and creative expression. We could gradually extend sensitivity of these various (internal) energies by practicing with improvisation groups. These body energies and active listening also connect consciously with the wider environment.

Ione was the "dream keeper" who imparted dream knowledge, enabling us to exercise awareness even in our sleeping hours. This knowledge was a powerful combination of her own spiritual and psychotherapy practice, and included many inspiring stories/experiences from North American indigenous people and other cultures in tune with dream worlds. Our work became a conscious effort to develop mind and body awareness 24 hours a day. It was surprising to note how the science and technology implemented in our waking hours appear in our dreams and if we train our dream technologies, then our creative play is unlimited. Recall how many scientists, inventors, mathematicians, etc. were inspired by something originating in something as "insubstantial" as the dream fabric of the night. Ione asked us to remind ourselves during waking hours "this is a dream". It is profound when one thinks how crazy our waking hours can be (as though having one's eyes open was something more "real" than a dream—but that is another debate…). Still, I found it disturbing to dream about Hotmail—the mundane daytime is sometimes a nightmare in itself.

Cut the Cosmic—Gimme der Computer

Perhaps a Deep Listening Workshop-Retreat is not quite what one may expect from an innovator of "new music". If we change this notion to "new listening", then it may not be the anomaly it…err…sounds.

Composers who work with computers and other electronic means create some extraordinary varieties of "new listening". This is the point. A tremendous knowledge bank is gained by entering more deeply into a profound study of psychoacoustics and studio-created listen-able (and non-audible yet perceptible) phenomena. In 1961 John Cage wrote: "New Music—New Listening". It is not something passé for its active practice is ever more urgent today. I recall a statement made out of sheer frustration at the Australian Computer Music Conference 1998 in Canberra: "If I hear another obvious computer sound—blip blip squigget squigget—I'll scream. I might as well get a microphone and record Nature".

To listen with awareness is not about entertaining silence, parking the bot, being unproductive. Like other meditation forms—it is work. It informs us. The following was a not-often-told anecdote of one the most-often-told Cage yarns.[60] Oliveros explained at the retreat:

When John Cage went into this room [an anechoic chamber] he heard a high sound, and a low sound. And the story went that the high sound was the sound of his nervous system and the low sound was the sound of his blood going through the veins. Well—that's the story. However, there is more to that story that is not generally known. John Cage died of a massive stroke just before his 80th birthday. A physician has said that you wouldn't hear blood pressure the way John described it. There was plaque in the arteries building up and that if someone had taken heed of what he had said, they would have known it was building towards a stroke. That was one thing. The other—the nervous system does not make a twang that you can hear like that either—it was also part of the condition that led to John Cage's stroke. So that is another part of the story that hasn't been told.

This was one of the many stories about listening and its power to tune into the very finest elements of our inner and outer environment. Aural attentiveness can lead to great discoveries. There is an ever-exciting interest in the nexus between consciousness, culture and technology.

Albeit "differently," this nexus has been the interest of many artists for a long time as Oliveros reminds us in her book, "Software for People":

By the end of the 50's, I was working with electronic means, and the whole field time and sound became my material, as John Cage has predicted for composers in his Credo of 1937. A most important discovery and major influence on my work occurred about 1958. This discovery came with the aid of technology.[61]

This galvanized a determination to expand listening. And this is what the DL retreat was all about. An integration of mind and bodywork to get in touch with the environment and our fellow humans, and to keep expanding listening, beyond and beyond, on and on. The DL trainers are totally enthused by the "technologies of consciousness" and, as did Cage, have a keen interest in working with Western science. We are in the process of finding a common language between the Eastern technologies of consciousness and Western science and technology. And most importantly, a practice entrenched with experience—not mere theory.

As an example of science confirming what Eastern mystics have known for centuries to be the benefits of meditation/relaxation, we were referred to the ECG frequency spectra of a heart in appreciation and frustration. See:
http://www.heartmath.com/freezeframer/science_of_freezeframer.html

Value for Ears and Heart

One could never claim isolation. The absence of hierarchy permitted genuine attention for each participant. Encouraging composers, especially women, seems to be something the trainers have done for years and destined to continue, yes, into the next millennium!. The Swiss women voiced how rare it is to be considered as composers (rather than "just" performers or teachers). But that can change. A classical singer had her chance (and space) to sing Mozart AND was overjoyed in scribing her first "experimental" composition for voices. Utilizing dissimilar voices (her own operatic quality, with the very different vocal qualities of performers like Vivienne Corringham and myself) she composed a piece evolved from a Tarot card. Being partial to spontaneous unpreparedness, I challenged the comment of a Swiss classical violinist, Christine Ragaz, who sighed how she always wanted to do something "experimental and improvised". I said, "Got your violin?" Despite the protest of "What! No rehearsal?" to be expected from the classically trained about to entertain public performance, she did take up my challenge. We performed a short but sweet spontaneity that made the heart sing.[62]

The workshop encouraged participants to take things learnt from the Retreat into the community. Skills can be transformed and applied to our everyday "reality". One male participant was enthused at his idea to begin a choir in Archen (Germany) consisting of people who "cannot sing". Gratitude was deeply felt by another male participant for the "woman energy". Although seemingly shy, he performed a gorgeous five-part piece complete with guitar, voice—even stones! He works as a music therapist with violent men so one can imagine the positive consequences of bringing the various subtleties of experience gained into that arena!

DL is about listening and interaction. And practice. Being mindful. 24 hours a day. It is about bringing it to the community as one's particular performance/training/creative offering. Artistic endeavor here promotes interconnectedness to other living systems—not being precious, but sharing our precious qualities.

Deep Listening was the uncanny fulfillment of the closing sentence of my first Master's sub-thesis:

> …difference is not the point, rather, listening differently in order to hear a more expansive sound art.

NOTE:

The writer extends her heartfelt thanks to Warren Burt and Martin Wesley-Smith who always encourage the humanity inherent in our work, and encouraged her meeting with Oliveros.

Caterina's attendance at the Deep Listening Retreat was partly assisted by ANAT—the Australian Network for Art and Technology's Conference & Workshop Fund, a devolved grant program of the Australia Council (the Australian Federal Government's Arts Funding and Advisory Body).

Deep Listening Koans and the Wizard of Oz

Maika Yuri Kusama

There is a famous Zen koan, a koan about the sound of one hand clapping. Have you heard it? I'm almost sure that you have! The sound of one hand clapping can only be heard within the realm of practicing deep listening. It is the direct experience of sound, eternal. It is the experience of no sound being filled—and obnoxious decibels being empty. It is the two in one, and the one in none.

Over the past few months I have used my meditation on deep listening and journal writing in Dr. Pauline Oliveros' class as a way in which to meditate on the interconnectedness of all sound, thus in essence digesting the sound of one hand. On the other hand I have been able to explore the thread of sound, its arrival and cessation. I have meditated on the healing aspects of sound, and universal dimensions of sound.

I really appreciated that we were a small group, coming together to a small music room on the Mills college campus to meditate on, elaborate on, collaborate on, and think about the phenomenon of listening and sound. *"Who'd think you'd find a group of college students meditating on a stained grey carpet in the old Mills music building, led by a white haired wise woman staring down at you from a projected computer image via satellite from New York. It is the Wizard of Oz come to life, what we've all imagined, larger than life."63*

Soon I could come to rely on our class as a sanctuary in the regular fast pace of things. Our chi-gung, visualizations and vocalizations are healing practices. I could see all the miniature shifts in the senses. *"It became obvious to me that the undercurrent of sound-or the sound of silence-can be reinterpreted as the container in which all sound arises and falls back into. Healing happens when this container becomes your body, and all sounds become your home."64* I became very interested in how sounds can be the gateway into a heightened awareness of the moment. Over and over again listening, following, becoming, and dropping. Using our body, our vessel to experience the depths of the senses.

For the first month of class all you could hear during the meditation was the sound of the lawnmowers and weedwackers. While sitting quietly you could sense the tension these machines brought. As the weeks went by it seems collectively that the group had kind of let the idea of sound nuisance go. Our acceptance for sound **as is** became obvious in the body language of the group during meditation. Ironically around this time the mowers stopped, and for the first time I realized what an inspiration loud decibels can be if used as tools to enter the moment time and time again.

In the Blue Cliff Records case 79 is entitled, "All Sounds." A monk and a teacher named Toshi have a little exchange about sound:
A monk asked Toshi, Is it true that All sounds are the voice of Buddha?"
Toshi said, "Yes."

The monk said, "Don't fart."
Toshi hit him.
Another question was, "Is it true that 'Course words and fine speech all end up in ultimate truth?"
Toshi said, "Yes."
The monk said, "Can I call you an ass?"
Toshi hit him.[65]

While this koan seems to deal with lively entrapment and humorous discourse, I thought it was also pointing to the fact that all sound is totally interconnected, spontaneous, and impermanent. One day during our meditation I wrote a spontaneous poem about sound. It was after Pauline had mentioned to me in an email the sound of the ocean current that researchers are currently documenting. It goes like this:

I'll send a strand
Out on a lit paper bird
Invoking Rays
To be the eyes out on the floor
Like an ivory pearl for you*
The siren bell within
Remembering the dance of 16 below C

That will come on—
In wavelengths⁓⁓ ⁓⁓ ⁓⁓⁓ ⁓⁓ ⁓ ⁓ ⁓ ⁓ ⁓ ⁓ ⁓ ⁓ ⁓ ⁓ ⁓ ⁓ ⁓⁓ ⁓ ⁓ ⁓ ⁓

We had been meditating as a group for over a month. The projection of Pauline (herself) on the wall, and the video camera were old friends. It was easy to slip into the sounds the moment had to offer. On this day, *"the scratchy sound of the reverb on Pauline's video chat was the constant rhythmic overtone, like freeway white noise. I sat on the floor cross legged*

and there are small moments of bliss-where there is just a free exchange that is really happening 24/7."[66]

This class has taught us to be more natural. This class has taught us to never mock the mundane and to expect the unexpected. That the unexpected is the mundane, and the expected…well, it's a figment of our imagination. In "Yunmen's Sound and Form," case 82 in the Book of Serenity, the introduction says:

"Not cutting off sound and form is falling wherever you are; searching by way of sound and looking by way of form, you don't see the Buddha. Isn't there anyone who can take to the road and return home?"

Then the case proceeds like this:

"Yunmen said to the assembly, 'Hearing sound, awaken to the way: seeing form, understand the mind. The Bodhisattva Avalokiteshvara brings money to buy a sesame cake: when he lowers his hand, it turns out to be a jelly doughnut."[67]

It is the surprise of the jelly doughnut, and the eternal jungle pulse of the multi-dimensional one hand that is forever certain in all its perfect and puzzling uncertainty. It is the magic of our life.

I am very grateful to have had the opportunity to experience Dr. Pauline Oliveros' **Deep Listening** class. It opened the door for a group of people to come together in regular daily life, to meditate on the root of sound, grow roots into the ground, embrace the mower, and embody the fact we really need to look no further than right under our very noses. Our dimensions are dancing*.

WEBLIOGRAPHY

http://www.deeplistening.org/pauline
This is the Pauline Oliveros' personal web page

http://www.deeplistening.org/
This is about the Pauline Oliveros Foundation programs and projects at Deep Listening Space in Kingston NY. POF is a non-profit arts organization.

http://www.deeplistening.org/Ione
Ione teaches with the instructor in the Deep Listening Retreats each summer. She is the author of *This is a Dream: A Handbook for Deep Dreamers*.

http://users.drew.edu/nlowrey/
Composer and mask maker Norman Lowrey is a Deep Listening Certificate holder. This web page details his singing masks.

http://interact.uoregon.edu/MediaLit/wfae/resources/index_resources.html
World Forum on Acoustic Ecology—there are many resources on this site concerning environmental recording and composing that will be used in assignments.

http://www.listen.org/
International Listening Association. Contains exercises and other information.

http://www.metatronpress.com/tbickley/resources/dlr.html
A reading list related to listening

http://www.deeplistening.org/news/
Dougherty,Tom Ed., Deep Listening Newsletter, Deep Listening Publications 1994 & 1995

http://www.advancedyogapractices.com/
Lessons In Yoga Practice

http://www.extensionyoga.com/
See Principle #7: The Importance of Yoga Breathing

http://aiki-jutsu.com/Page7Zen.htm

http://www.shalem.org/walk.html

http://www.lloydwatts.com/
Information on reverse engineering the auditory pathway in the brain

http://www.neurophys.wisc.edu/aud/training.html
Links for auditory training and education

BIBLIOGRAPHY

Andrews, Ted, *Sacred Sounds*: *Transformation through Music & Word*, St. Paul: Llewellyn Publications (1994)

Beaulieu, John, *Music and Sound in the Healing Arts*, Barrytown: Station Hill (1987)

Berendt, Joachim-Ernst, *The World Is Sound-Nada Brahma*, Rochester VT: Destiny Books (1983)

Berendt, Joachim-Ernst, *The Third Ear*, New York, Henry Holt (1985)

Benson, Herbert, MD & Proctor, William, *The Breakout Principle: How to activate the natural trigger that maximizes creativity, athletic performance, productivity and personal well-being.* Scribner (2003)

Benson, Herbert, MD, *The Relaxation Response*, Harper & Collins (1975)

Benzon, William, *Beethoven's Anvil: Music in Mind and Culture*, Basic Books (2001)

Bonny, Helen L./Savary, Louis M., *Music & Your Mind: Listening with a New Consciousness*, Barrytown: Station Hill (1990)

Breathnach, Sarah Ban, *Simple Abundance, A Daybook of Comfort and Joy* Warner Books (1995)

Bush, Carol A., *Healing Imagery and Music: Pathways to the Inner Self,* Portland: Rudra Press (1995)

Cage, John, *Silence,* Middletown, Wesleyan University Press (1965)

Calvin, William H., *How Brains Think: Evolving Intelligence, Then and Now,* Basic Books (1997)

Calvin, William H & Bickerton, Derek, *Lingua ex Machina: Reconciling Darwin and Chomsky with the Human Brain*, MIT Press (2001)

Campbell, Don, *Music and Miracles*, compilation, Wheaton: Quest Books (1992)

Campbell, Don, *Music Physician for the Times to Come*, compilation, Wheaton: Quest Books (1991)

Campbell, Don, *The Roar of Silence*, Wheaton: Quest Books (1989)

Cardew, Carnelius, *Scratch Music*, Cambridge: MIT Press (1975)

Cook, Perry R., Ed. *Music, Cognition, and Computerized Sound: An Introduction to Psychoacoustics*, MIT Press (1999)

Dadson, Philip & McGlashan, Don, *The From Scratch Rhythm Workbook*, Revised Edition, Heineman (1995)

Devall, Bill, Sessions, George, *Deep Ecology: Living As If Nature Mattered*, Peregrine Smith Books, (1985)

D'Olivet, Fabre, *Music Explained as Science and Art and Considered in its Analogical Relations to Religious Mysteries, Ancient Mythology and The History of the World*, Inner Traditions International, (1987)

Fontana, David & Slack, Ingrid, *Teaching Meditation to Children: A Practical Guide to the use and benefits of meditation techniques*, Element Books (1997)

Goldman, Jonathan, *Healing Sounds: The Power of Harmonics*, Rockport MA: Element (1992)

Gardner, Kay, *Sounding the Inner Landscape: Music as Medicine,* Stonington: Caduceus (1990)

Garfield, Leah Maggie, *Sound Medicine: Healing with Music, Voice and Song*, Berkeley: Celestial Arts (1987)

Greenfield, Susan A., *Journey to the Centers of the Mind: Toward a Science of Consciousness*, Freeman Press (1995)

Hanh, Thich Nhat, *The Long Road Turns To Joy*, Unified Buddhist Church (1995)

Hanh, Thich Nhat, Foreword by H.H. the Dalai Lama, *Peace Is Every Step: The Path of Mindfulness in Everyday Life*, Rider (1995)

Halpern, Steven, Sound *Health: The Music and Sounds That Make Us Whole*, San Francisco: Harper and Row (1985)

Hamel, Peter Michael, *Through Music to the Self*, Boulder: Shambala (1978)

Listening: An Introduction to the Perception of Auditory Eventss, Handel, Stephen, MIT Press (1989)

Hardison, O.B., *Disappearing Through the Skylight: Culture and Technology in the Twentieth Century*, Penguin Books (1989)

Ione, *Listening in Dreams: A Compendium of Dreams, Meditations and Rituals for Deep Dreamers*, Deep Listening Publications (2003)

Ione, *This Is A Dream: A Handbook for Deep Dreamers*, M.O.M. Press (2001)

Jenny, Hans, *Cymatics: The Structure and Dynamics of Waves and Vibrations,* Vol. I & II Basel Switzerland: Basilius Press (1967)

Khan,Sufi Hazrat Inayat, *Music*, Samuel Weiser (1962)

Leonard, George, *The Silent Pulse*, New York: Bantam New Age Books (1981)

Lewis, Dennis, *Free Your Breath, Free Your Life: How Conscious Breathing Can Relieve Stress, Increase Vitality and Help You to Live More Fully*, Shambala (2004)

Linklater, Kristin, *Freeing the Natural Voice*, New York: Drama Books (1976)

Mathieu, W.A, *The Listening Book: Discovering Your Own Music*, Shambala (1991)

McClelland Ph.D., Randall, *The Healing Forces of Music: History, Theory and Practice*, Element (1991)

MacInerney, Charles et al. *Expanding Paradigms*, Austin, TX (1989)

Metzner, Jim, *Pulse of the Planet: Extraordinary Sounds From the Natural World* The Nature Company stores and catalog (1995)

Mindell, Arnold, *The Deep Democracy of Open Forums: Practical Steps to Conflict Prevention and Resolution for the Family, Workplace, and World*, Hampton Books (2002)

Nyman, Michael, *Experimental Music_Cage and Beyond*, New York: Schirmer Books (1974)

Oliveros, Pauline, *Deep Listening: A Composer's Sound Practice, Deep Listening Publications, (2003)*

Oliveros, Pauline, *Deep Listening Pieces*, Deep Listening Publications 1990

Oliveros, Pauline, *Software for People: Essays from 1963-1980*, Smith Publications 1984

Oliveros, Pauline, *Sonic Meditations*, Smith Publications 1973 or Source Magazine

Oliveros, Pauline, *The Roots of the Moment*, Drogue Press (1999)

Ornstein, Robert, *Multimind: A New Way of Looking at Human Behavior*, Doubleday, (1986)

Ornstein, Robert, *The Nature of Human Consciousness: A Book of Readings,* Freeman (1973)

Ornstein, Robert, *Evolution of Consciousness: The Origin of the Way We Think,* Touchtone (1991)

Ornstein, Robert, Erhlich, Paul, *New World New Mind: A Brilliantly Original Guide to Changing the Way*, Simon Schuster (1989)

Paynter, John and Aston, Peter, *Sound and Silence: Classroom Projects in Creative Music*, London: Cambridge University Press (1970)

Pert, Candace, *Molecules of Emotion: The Science Behind Mind-Body Medicine,* Touchstone *(1997)*

Pinkel, Benjamin, *Consciousness, Matter and Energy: The Emergence of Mind in Nature*, Turover Press (1992)

Rudhyar, Dane, *The Magic of Tone and the Art of Music*, Boulder: Shambala (1982)

Schafer, R. Murray, *Our Sonic Environment and the Soundscape the Tuning of the World*, Destiny Books, Rochester, Vermont, (1994)

Schwenk, Theodore, *Sensitive Chaos: The Creation of Flowing Forms in Water & Air*, New York: Schocken Books (1976)

Scott, Cyrill, *Music: It's Secret Influence Through the Ages*, London: Theosophical Publishing House (1937)

Smith, Leo, *Notes (8 pieces) Source a new world music: Creative music*, Leo Smith (1973)

Stevens, S.S. and Warhofsky, F., *Sound and Hearing*, New York: Time-Life Books, (1965)

Stewart, R.J., *The Spiritual Dimension of Music: Altering Conscious for Inner Development*, Rochester VT: Destiny Books (1987)

Strogatz, Steven, *SYNC: The Emerging Science of Spontaneous Order*, Theia (2003)

Tame, David, *The Secret Power of Music*, New York: Destiny (1984)

Thiel, Phillip, *People, Paths, and Purposes: Notations for a Participatory Envirotecture*, University of Washington Press (1997)

Thompson, Emily, *The Soundscape of Modernity:Architectural Acoustics and the Culture of Listening in America 1900-1933*, MIT Press (2002)

Tulku, Tarthang, *Kum Nye Relaxation.* Nyingama Psycholoy Series, (1979)

Zuckernandl, Victor, *Sound and Symbol: Music and the External World*, Princeton: Princeton University Press (1969)

GLOSSARY

Some of the words used in Deep Listening practice are borrowed from other disciplines. Some of these words such as Chakra and Chi have passed into popular use in English and are to be found in dictionaries. T'ai Chi, Chi Kung and Yoga are now taught and practiced widely in the United States. Chi is often spelled as Qi. The "Pinyin" system is the official Romanization system of Chinese but be aware that Chinese transliteration varies in general Romanized English.

Chakra—an energy center in the body. Recognized in yoga as a center of spiritual power.

Chi—Energy or life force in Chinese medicine and philosophy. Chi is the energy of the universe that flows through and around all living things. See *Science and Civilization in China* by Joseph Needham.

Chi Kung—A series of exercises designed to build Chi in the body. See Qi Qong.

Dan T'ien—the lower energy center (below the navel).

Lotus position—a particular posture of the body used in meditation where one is seated on the floor with legs crossed, feet on thighs, and back straight.

Mantra—a word or phrase that is repeated during meditation to assist in one's development of spiritual power.

Qi Qong—Qi means energy and Qong is development. See Chi Kung.

Soundscape—a term coined by R. Murray Schaefer analogous to landscape—or what is sounding in the surrounding environment of the listener.

T'ai Chi—Chinese physical exercises featuring forms of slow and flowing circular movements of the limbs and torso. There are many styles of T'ai Chi for example Yang or Wu style. The style practiced by Heloise Gold in the Deep Listening Retreats is Yang.

Yoga—a spiritual practice consisting of rituals, postures, and breathing exercises designed to bring about a feeling of unity with a divine being.

REFERENCES

1 The CD *"Deep Listening"* (NA 022), subsequently released on New Albion Records in spring 1989, not only garnered several spectacular reviews, but was also named among the ten best jazz recordings of the year by Pulse! magazine.

2 See http://www.newmusicbox.org/news/may00/obit_ldlugoszewski.html, http://www.artofthestates.org/cgi-bin/piece.pl?pid=15, and http://musicmavericks.publicradio.org/features/interview_dlugoszewski.html

3 Soundscape is a term coined by Canadian composer R. Murray Schaefer in his book *The Tuning of the World*, A pioneering exploration into the past history and present state of the most neglected aspect of our environment: The Soundscape, Knopf, 1977.

4 **Robert Erickson** (1917-1997) was born in Marquette, Michigan, where as a youth he played violin, piano and flute. Drawn to composition in his teenage years, he found his principal teacher in Ernst Krenek, whom he met in Chicago in 1938. He followed Krenek to Hamline University in St. Paul, Minnesota, and studied with him until 1947 (with three years of Army service in between). Erickson's other teachers included May Strong, Wesley La Violette, and Roger Sessions. He began his own teaching career at the College of St. Catherine in St. Paul, Minnesota, then held a series of positions at San Francisco State College, University of California at Berkeley, San Francisco Conservatory, and University of California at San Diego, whose music department he co-founded with Wilbur Ogden in 1967. Among Erickson's honors are fellowships from the Ford and Guggenheim Foundations, and election as a Fellow of the Institute for Creative Arts of the University of California (1968). He wrote a number of books and articles on diverse topics such as ancient tuning systems and the relationship between phonetics and music; his most recent work was **Sound Structure in Music** (1975).

5 To improvise means to create music spontaneously while vocalizing or performing on a musical instrument. Often while composing I would improvise several versions of a phrase, phrases or a section at the piano.

6 *"Variations for Sextet* is an example of Oliveros' early "traditional" works. It bears the influence of her mentor and teacher, Robert Erickson, a prominent author of acoustic theory and advocate of intuitive compositional methods.

Oliveros stated that although her earliest works were composed using conventional musical notation and tend to sound like the works of Anton Webern, she created them by improvising rather than applying a rigorous intellectual technique. Written for flute/piccolo, Bb clarinet, Bb trumpet, F horn, 'cello, and piano, Variations explores her interest in timbre or sound color through her use of timbral gestures, rapid shifts in tone color, and radical shifts in rhythm." Program note from *Sounding the Margins a Forty Year Retrospective* produced by Meridian Gallery, Anne Brodzky, director and Pauline Oliveros Foundation Bay Area at the Lorraine Hansberry Theater in San Francisco.

7   *I of IV* for tape was performed in real time in the Electronic Music Studio at the University of Toronto in the summer of 1966. *I of IV* was released in 1967 on Odyssey Records and reissued on Paradigm in1997. For technical information see *Tape Delay Techniques for Electronic Music Composers* in *Software for People,* Pauline Oliveros, Smith Publications/ Printed Editions 1984.

8   *Bye Bye Butterfly* is a two channel tape composition made at the San Francisco Tape Music Center. It utilizes two Hewlett Packard oscillators; two line amplifiers in cascade, a turntable with record and two tape recorders in a delay setup. The composer arranged the equipment, tuned the oscillators, and played through the composition in real time.
"*Bye Bye Butterfly* bids farewell not only to the music of the 19th century but also to the system of polite morality of that age and its attendant institutionalized oppression of the female sex. The title refers to the operatic disc, *Madame Butterfly* by Giacomo Puccini, which was at hand in the studio at the time and which was spontaneously incorporated into the ongoing compositional mix." *Bye Bye Butterfly* is included in *Ohm the Early Gurus of Electronic Music*, Ellipsis Arts, 2000 and was first released in 1977 on *New Music for Electronic and Recorded Media*, 1750 Arch Records, reissued subsequently by CRI 1997 and on Paradigm 1997.

9   John Rockwell, Archives of the New York Times, Ten Best Pieces of Electronic Music of the Decade December, 1969

10   *The Nature of Music* was a course for the general student at the University of California intended to introduce music through creative participation. Students composed performed and improvised music.

11   *A New Music Education for Everyman in Experiment & Innovation: New Directions in Education.* The University of California, Volume 1, Number 2, January 1968 by Wilbur Ogden

12 *Sonic Meditations*, Smith Publications (1971) is a collection of verbally notated meditations that may be enjoyed by anyone in a variety of ways: read as poetry, performed alone or performed for an audience

13 See *Attention*, Chapter 15 *Zen and the Brain*, James F. Austin M.D., MIT Press 1999

14 *Source: Music of the Avant Garde* (1967-1972) (Out of print. A few single issues are still available from the Deep Listening Catalog, http://www/deeplistening.org/dlc.)
A semi-annual anthology of scores, articles and LP recordings. Only 11 issues, Volumes 1-6, produced. Extant issues: 4-11 (except for #5). Editors include Larry Austin, Stanley Lunetta, John Cage, Alvin Lucier, and Ken Friedman. Available in various quantities per extant issue. Printed on high quality paper, with 4-color reproductions, 11" by 14", spiral bound; LP recordings included in 4 issues.

15 *Software for People: Essays from 1962-1980, Pauline Oliveros, Smith Publications/ Printed Editions*—includes articles on new music, women as composers, sonic meditation, attention and awareness, and technique. (1984)

16 Project for Music Experiment directed by Roger Reynolds (1973-1975) was an organized research unit established by the faculty of the Music Department of the University of California at San Diego. It later became the Center for Music Experiment and Related Research, directed by Pauline Oliveros from 1976 to 1979.

17 *Meditation Project* was my research in the Project for Music Experiment. See *Meditation Project, Software for People*, ibid.

18 My meditation studies included Kinetic Awareness with Elaine Summers in New York NY; T'ai Chi Ch'uan with Al Chung Liang Huang in Rancho Santa Fe CA and Heloise Gold at Rose Mountain Retreat Center, Las Vegas NM; Shotokan Karate with Lester Ingber at the Institute for the Study of Attention in Solano Beach CA; Za Zen practice with John Daido Loori at Zen Mountain Center, Mt. Tremper NY; Tibetan Buddhist Shine practice from H.E. T'ai Situ Rinpoche at Karma Triyana Dharma Chakra in Woodstock NY; Yoga meditation from Dr. Rammurti S. Mishra at Ananda Ashram in Monroe NY; and Chi Kung from Taoist Master T.K. Hsih in Kingston NY.

19 Rose Mountain Retreat Center, Las Vegas NM, Andy Gold proprietor

20 T'ai Chi, is an ancient Chinese discipline of slow, graceful meditative movements practiced as a system of exercises. There are many different styles of

T'ai Chi forms. Examples are Yang and Wu styles named for the family that practiced or developed the form. T'ai Chi is also a form of martial art.

21 Chi Kung or Qi Qong: A series of exercises designed to build Chi in the body. Chi or Qi is energy or life force in Chinese medicine and philosophy. Chi is the energy of the universe that flows through and around all living things. See *Science and Civilization in China* by Joseph Needham. Kung or Qong means development.

22 *Listening Through Dreaming: A Handbook for Deep Dreamers* by Ione, Deep Listening Publications 2004

23 Deep Listening in Switzerland was organized by Margrit Schenker and held at Hotel Regina in the high Alps in Muerren in 1998, 1999, and at the Kulturhotel Seeguetli in 2001. Subsequently Christine Zehnder-Probst organized two more retreats at the Kulturhotel Seguetli n 2004 and 2005.

24 Deep Listening Haliburton was organized by Gayle Young and held in the Haliburton Wildlife Preserve at Stocking Lake, Ontario in the summer of 2000.

25 Deep Listening at Cloud Mountain was organized by Robert Mann and held at Cloud Mountain Retreat Center in Washington State in 1994.

26 The Three Year Certificate program is offered through Deep Listening Retreats to prepare the participant to teach Deep Listening Workshops. See http://www.deeplistening.org for the requirements of this program

27 The first Three Year Certificates were awarded to Tom Bickley, Anne Bourne, Abbie Conant, Norman Lowrey, Dominique Mazeaud and Kimberly McCarthy,

28 See *Brain Stimulation in the Study of Neuronal Functions for Conscious Sensory Experiences: Subjective Referral of Sensory Experience Backward in Time* by Benjamin Libet in *Essential Sources in the Scientific Study of Consciousness*, Edited by Bernard J. Baars, William P. Banks and James B. Newman, MIT Press 2003

29 Deep Listening at Rensselaer Polytechnic Institute is taught in the fall and spring semesters as an upper division course for undergraduates and graduates. There are no prerequisites for the course.

30 Deep Listening at Mills College is taught in the fall as an upper division course for undergraduates and graduates without prerequisites. I teach the Course through *virtual presence* using iCHATav for MacIntosh computer after an initial physical visit. I appear in the Mills College classroom on a large screen and can see and hear the students and give instruction from my home in Kingston New York.

31 See *Strategies and Models of Selective Attention* by Anne M. Triesman, in *Essential Sources in the Scientific Study of Consciousness*, Edited by Bernard J. Baars, William P. Banks and James B. Newman, MIT Press 2003

32 See *Introduction: Treating Consciousness as a Variable: The Fading Taboo* in *Essential Sources in the Scientific Study of Consciousness*, Edited by Bernard J. Baars, William P. Banks and James B. Newman, MIT Press 2003

33 See *Brain Stimulation in the Study of Neuronal Functions for Conscious Sensory Experiences: Subjective Referral of Sensory Experience Backward in Time* by Benjamin Libet in *Essential Sources in the Scientific Study of Consciousness*, Edited by Bernard J. Baars, William P. Banks and James B. Newman, MIT Press 2003

34 See *The Audible Past*, Jonathan Sterne, Duke University Press, 2003, pg 96

35 See Chapter 1, *A Point of View* in *Listening: An Introduction to the Perception of Auditory Events*, Stephen Handel, MIT Press, 1993

36 Stephen Handel in *Listening: An Introduction to the Perception of Auditory Events,* ibid.

37 Dr. Ros Bandt
http://www.sounddesign.unimelb.edu.au/site/NationPaper/NationPaper.html

38 *Bodymind* is used by Candace Pert in her *Molecules of Emotion: The Science Behind Mind-Body Medicine* and James L. Oschman in *Energy Medicine in Therapeutics and Human Performance*, Bodymind expresses the continuum of the living matrix, that there is no separation between mind and body.

39 See http://www.plumvillage.org/tnh/embracing_anger.htm *Embracing Anger*, A Public Talk by Thich Nhat Hanh at the Riverside Church, New York—September 25th, 2001.

40 Energy flows in the body include electricity, heat and magnetism. See *Energy Medicine: The Scientific Basis of Bioenergetic Therapies* by James L. Oschmann PhD. With an introduction by Candace Pert, Churchill Livingstone 2002.

41 Process training emphasizes action rather than goals or product. There is an overview of Deep Listening that can only be understood by experiencing the exercises. Process is initiated by action and is observed by the doer. The result is experience and understanding through experience.

42 There are numerous points that are found along the acupuncture meridians throughout the body and associated with different organs of the body. See http://www.acumedico.com/kidney.htm Bubbling brook or kidney point http://www.chinesemedicinesampler.com/acupuncture.html http://www.qi-journal.com/tcmarticles/acumodel/listpoints.asp

43 The Taoist number system is based on early Taoist numerology. See http://www.springtimesong.com/wcFeature108.htm A Closer Look at the Number 108 by Ray Van Raamsdonk

44 Sympathetic nervous system—See http://faculty.washington.edu/chudler/auto.html

45 Parasympathetic nervous system—See http://faculty.washington.edu/chudler/auto.html

46 http://www.extensionyoga.com/ See Principle # 7: *The Importance of Yoga Breathing*

47 See *Free Your Breath, Free Your Life: How Conscious Breathing Can Relieve Stress, Increase Vitality and Help You to Live More Fully*, Dennis Lewis, Shambala (2004)

48 See http://www.uwec.edu/greider/Buddha/Buddhism.Course/Students_Projects_Sites/baehring.sitting%20and%20meditation/sitting_aspect_of_meditation.htm Also see http://tekishin.org/zazen/zazeneg.htm.

49 Mantra is a Word, phrase or sound that is repeated during meditation. Mantra means "instrument of thought: according to the *Cologne Digital Lexicon.—* http://www.uni-koeln.de/phil-fak/indologie/tamil/mwd_search.html

50 See Jonathan Sterne, *The Audible Past*, Duke University Press, 2003, pg 97

51 From a conversation with Ramon Sender Barayon.

52 The balancing of Yin and Yang is related to masculine and feminine energy thus the left hand is Yin and the right hand Yang. This is the reason for specifying which hand to use.

53 In the Chinese system of Chi Kung and T'ai Chi the dan t'ien is the lower energy center just beneath the navel.

54 See http://www.chclibrary.org/micromed/00063360.html Reflexology

55 See http://home.pacbell.net/brodsky/nails.html The Mechanics of the Three Nails: Develop your root—

56 See http://history.acusd.edu/gen/recording/notes.html Recording Technology History notes revised Feb. 16, 2004, by Steve Schoenherr

57 For very basic information see http://www.ehow.com/how_10021_record-sound-windows.html How to Record a Sound on a Windows Computer.

58 There are many freeware and shareware recording editing programs. For the projects in this book I recommend the open source freeware program Audacity. Audacity works on both DOS and MACos platforms.

59 Never-never: colloquial Australian for sparsely inhabited desert country; a remote and isolated region, especially that of inland Australia; an imaginary land

60 Yarn: colloquial Australian for "story telling".

61 Oliveros, Pauline, *Software for People*, p 182.

62 My character was the ghost of Cathy Berberian. Later Ione invited me to act in a film where I play Carla Gregarian, a vocalist ghost. An outline of this can be found on the Deep Listening website as one of their Projects. This thirty-minute video opera was initially titled Hotel Regina where this retreat took place in Muerren.

63 Deep Listening class journal, Maika Yuri Kusama, 9-20-04

64 Deep listening Journal, Maika Yuri Kusama, 10-11-04

65 *Secrets of the Blue Cliff Record*, Zen comments by Hauin and Tenkei, Shambala, Boston and London, 2002.

66 Deep Listening Journal, 9-27-04

67 *The Book of Serenity*, translation by Thomas Cleary, 1990, The Lindasfarne Press, Hudson, NY.

INDEX

0-595-34365-1

91904178R00078

Made in the USA
Middletown, DE
03 October 2018